Skateboarding and Femininity

Skateboarding and Femininity explores and highlights the value of femininity both within skateboarding and wider culture. This book examines skateboarding's relationship to gender politics through a consideration of the personal politics connected to individual skateboarders, the social-spatial arenas in which skateboarding takes place, and by understanding the performance of tricks and symbolic movements as part of gender-based power dynamics. Dani Abulhawa analyses the discursive frameworks connected to skateboarding philanthropic projects and how these operate through gendered tropes. Through the author's work with skateboarding charity SkatePal, this book offers an alternative way of recognising the value of skateboarding philanthropy projects, proposing a move toward a more open and explorative somatic practice perspective.

Dani Abulhawa is a Senior Lecturer in Performance at Sheffield Hallam University, an ambassador for skateboarding charity SkatePal, and a committed amateur skateboarder. Dani has authored articles and chapters and created performances exploring skateboarding, play, and dance/performance in relation to the personal-bodily politics of place.

Routledge Advances in Theatre and Performance Studies

Closet Drama
History, Theory, Form
Edited by Catherine Burroughs

Contemporary Group Theatre in Kolkata, India
Arnab Banerji

Skateboarding and Femininity
Gender, Space-making and Expressive Movement
Dani Abulhawa

Dynamic Cartography
Body, Architecture, and Performative Space
Maria Jose Martinez Sanchez

Situated Knowing
Epistemic Perspectives on Performance
Edited by Ewa Bal and Mateusz Chaberski

Japanese Political Theatre in the 18th Century
Bunraku Puppet Plays in Social Context
Akihiro Odanaka and Masami Iwai

Aotearoa New Zealand in the Global Theatre Marketplace
James Wenley

For more information about this series, please visit: https://www.routledg e.com/Routledge-Advances-in-Theatre--Performance-Studies/book-series/ RATPS

Skateboarding and Femininity
Gender, Space-making and Expressive Movement

Dani Abulhawa

LONDON AND NEW YORK

First published 2020
by Routledge
2 Park Square, Milton Park, Abingdon, Oxon OX14 4RN

and by Routledge
52 Vanderbilt Avenue, New York, NY 10017

Routledge is an imprint of the Taylor & Francis Group, an informa business

© 2020 Dani Abulhawa

The right of Dani Abulhawa to be identified as author of this work has been asserted by her in accordance with sections 77 and 78 of the Copyright, Designs and Patents Act 1988.

All rights reserved. No part of this book may be reprinted or reproduced or utilised in any form or by any electronic, mechanical, or other means, now known or hereafter invented, including photocopying and recording, or in any information storage or retrieval system, without permission in writing from the publishers.

Trademark notice: Product or corporate names may be trademarks or registered trademarks, and are used only for identification and explanation without intent to infringe.

British Library Cataloguing-in-Publication Data
A catalogue record for this book is available from the British Library

Library of Congress Cataloging-in-Publication Data
A catalog record has been requested for this book

ISBN: 978-0-367-45759-4 (hbk)
ISBN: 978-0-367-50714-5 (pbk)
ISBN: 978-1-003-02574-0 (ebk)

Typeset in Times New Roman
by Deanta Global Publishing Services, Chennai, India

Contents

List of figures		vi
Acknowledgements		vii
	Introduction: Getting connected to who you are	1
1	Girls and women holding and creating space in skateboarding	16
2	Skateboarding and feminism	44
3	Skateboarding physical culture	62
4	'Skateboard philanthropy': A somatic practice perspective	81
	Conclusion: Skateboarding's participation in the world beyond itself	103
	Index	110

Figures

1.1 Laura Thornhill Caswell, one-foot nose wheelie, 1976. Image by James Mahoney   20

1.2 Laura Thornhill Caswell, full-pipe Arizona desert, 1976. Image by Warren Bolster   21

1.3 Lucy Adams, switch front shuv, wearing 'real girls skate curbs' Lovenskate t-shirt, 2015. Image by Chris Johnson   30

1.4 Lovenskate Devrim Zamani deck, 2015. Image by Nick Sharratt   32

1.5 Teigan Komaromi, street plant, 2019. Image by Jenna Selby   33

3.1 Joe Moore, nosegrab wedge plant escalator ride, taken in Shibuya of Tokyo, Japan while exploring the area with the Yabai clothing team. Image by Rena Kobayashi   64

4.1 Asira skatepark, view from top of flatbank, 2015. Image by Emil Agerskov   84

4.2 Local young people learning to skateboard in Asira Al-Shamalyia's Rosa Skatepark, 2015. Image by Emil Agerskov   85

4.3 View of the south side of Asira Al-Shamalyia's Rosa Skatepark, 2015. Image by Emil Agerskov   89

4.4 Push, 2019. Illustrated by Jon Horner   92

4.5 Ollie, 2019. Illustrated by Jon Horner   92

4.6 Drop In, 2019. Illustrated by Jon Horner   93

4.7 SkatePal volunteer assisting a hippy jump, 2017. Image by Emil Agerskov   94

4.8 View of northeast corner of Asira Al-Shamalyia's Rosa Skatepark, 2015. Image by Emil Agerskov   96

Acknowledgements

The ideas within this book have developed from a love of skateboarding that has persisted for what has become decades now. I am not a typical skateboarder and it has taken me a long time to become comfortable with being slightly out of place and to locate my own body and practice within this culture. This book is the result of a process of noticing and learning since my adolescence, of the conversations I have taken part in and the relationships I have been fortunate enough to have in adulthood. My first word of thanks must go to Laura Powell and Anna Bailey for your friendship and support, and for helping me to recognise what it means to make space for yourself as a woman and as a skateboarder.

I would probably not have developed the confidence to write this book if it wasn't for the skateboarder-writers – those who lurk message boards, those who write difficult articles – and the professional and amateur skateboarders who put themselves out there to start and support movements. With particular regard to this book, I would like to express my sincere thanks to Leo Baker, M. Dabbadie, Jilleen Liao, Anthony Pappalardo, Kyle Beachy, Chris Jones, and Ryan Lay. I am grateful for your progressive ideas and approach to social justice within the world of skateboarding (and beyond). Additionally, thanks to M, Anthony, and Chris for reading and providing feedback on some of the writing in the book.

Thank you to Jenna Selby for all the work you have done supporting women and girls in the UK, and to Dannii Gallagher for your work on Girl Skate UK and letting me write for the site. Thank you to Ben Powell for your inspiration, for what you and the team provided for British skateboarders through *Sidewalk*, and for your kind support and help with all my questions. I would also like to acknowledge the work of all the people I have written about in this book, particularly Leo Baker, Leticia Bufoni, Marissa Dal Santo, Elissa Steamer, and Tony Hawk.

Special thanks must go to the challenging, critical, and kind community of academics and non-academics that has developed in and through Re-verb and Pushing Boarders, and which is becoming a bourgeoning new field of viii *Acknowledgements*

enquiry and discourse. Especially Thom Callan-Riley, Sander Hölsgens, Chris Lawton, Adelina Ong, Paul O'Connor, Sophie Friedel, Indigo Willing, Åsa Bäckström, Jilleen Liao, Dwayne Dixon, Carrie Paechter, and Esther Sayers, each of whose work has directly impacted on the ideas in this book. Thom, Sander, and Chris – I am so grateful to work alongside you, for each of your expertise and for the rigour of our conversations. Thank you to the pioneers of skateboarding in academia, particularly Becky Beal and Iain Borden for impelling me to write about my own experiences. And especially to Iain for your continued guidance and support.

There are several people who have contributed to the book: thank you to Jon Horner for your illustrations, to Joe Moore for your inspirational and completely unique skateboarding practice, to Lucy Adams for supporting women in skateboarding and for your leadership, to Stuart Smith for everything you're doing with Lovenskate, to Cindy Whitehead for all your work supporting women and girls globally and for kindly giving your time to participate in my research. Thanks to Paola Ruiloba and Rachael Sherlock for each giving up some of your time to contribute to this book. Thanks also to Teigan Komaromi for granting permission to use your streetplant in the book, and to Chris Johnson, Nick Sharratt, Emil Agerskov, and again to Jenna Selby for your contribution of images. Special thanks to Laura Thornhill Caswell for such a wealth of experience, for giving up so much of your time for me to ask questions, and for providing such incredible images that capture an important part of the history of skateboarding.

To everyone involved with SkatePal who have supported the work featured in Chapter 4, particularly those people who have given up their time for interviews and offered their insights and comments in the town of Asira Al-Shamalyia, Shukran Jazeelan. Thanks especially to Charlie and Theo for the work you do and for letting me be a part of it, to Mohammed Sawalha, all the volunteers of SkatePal, and to Raya Aljundi for your interpreting work on the research.

This book is anchored to and supported by my background in performance. In this regard, I would like to express my ongoing thanks to my mentors and friends, Bob Whalley and Lee Miller, and Roberta Mock – for their continued guidance and insight. Thanks also to Roberta for your supportive feedback on Chapter 2.

Thank you to my parents, Veronika and Jamal, and my brothers, Faraz and Samir – for fostering an atmosphere of openness, support, and lightheartedness when I was growing up and growing into skateboarding that has allowed me the space to be myself with humility.

Finally, I would like to thank Christian Berger for your time reading and discussing so many of these ideas with me, for encouraging and challenging my perspectives, and for bringing a playfulness and lucidity to my life on and off the board.

Introduction

Getting connected to who you are

Within the realms of sport and physical activity, gender has traditionally been articulated through the limiting binary positions of masculinity and femininity and rigidly applied to biological markers of sex difference.[1] Together with post-structuralist discourse that sought to untangle the constructed and discursively produced connection between gender and sex (most notably in Butler 1990[2]), there has been in recent decades a growing popular interest in understanding and expanding these categories, through the terms 'non-binary' and 'genderqueer', amongst others.

Examinations of gender presentation have expanded considerably in this discursive climate toward more local and situated discussions of practice that illustrate broader presentations of gender. For example, Kath Woodward discusses gender identity in boxing by articulating how it is possible to go beyond the simple label of 'masculinity', and to see a rather more complex and fluid set of gender markers.[3] Similarly, Adele Pavlidis has examined the relatively recent resurgence of roller derby as a sport specifically aimed at women.[4] She discusses how roller derby incorporates an explicit parodying of hetero-normative gender relations. She writes, '[t]his is evidenced by the often overtly sexualised costumes commonly worn – such as fishnet stockings and garter belts – and the outrageous names used, such as 'Storm in a D Cup' and 'Annabella Apocalipstick''.[5] This view of sport and physical activity has also been discussed in Carolyn Ali Khan's articulation of her rollerblading practice as a 'site of resistance against the perfection of fossilized flat female norms'.[6] Skateboarding is an ambiguously defined cultural practice[7] that is generally regarded as a male-dominated activity.[8] But it is also one in which participants display alternative forms of masculinity.[9] These examples suggest that academic and populist discourse supports a turn away from binary gender categories in favour of a more accurate and nuanced examination of the human condition. Lynda Johnston, in her article examining gender diversity within the field of geography notes, 'at the heart of this debate is the desire to unsettle and disrupt gendered binaries by taking embodiment seriously'.[10]

2 Introduction

Skateboarding has since its beginnings been rooted in a practice of self-expression through movement and of developing an authentic sense of self through persistent and repeated bodily practice. Describing skateboarding in the 1960s, veteran professional skateboarder Stacey Peralta articulates how important style in performance has been to skateboarding. He explains,

> Style was the most important thing, because skateboarding wasn't technical back then, so [it was] the only thing you had going for you. ... You practiced maneuvers over and over and over again, because you wanted to get them connected to who you were. When you did a great Bertlemann turn, man... it was a gesture of who you were.[11]

This idea of skateboarding movement being connected to who you are is a popular concept, but one that has not been unpacked at length within skateboarding academia or populist sources. Skateboarder identity more generally has been elaborated through interviews and cultural artefacts within a range of populist books including those that offer a history or chronological overview of skateboarding, such as Michael Brooke's *History of Skateboarding*[12] or Jocko Weyland's *Skateboarder's History of the World*,[13] books that examine skateboarding culture, such as Sean Mortimer's *Stalefish*[14] or James Davis's *Skateboarding is Not a Crime*,[15] and those that focus on women's and girl's skateboarding, particularly Patty Segovia and Rebecca Heller's *Skater Girl: A Girl's Guide to Skateboarding*[16] and Natalie Porter's self-published *The History of Women in Skateboarding*.[17] Skateboarder identity has also been critically examined in academic sources spanning approx. the last 25 years and beginning most notably with the work of Becky Beal[18] and Iain Borden[19] throughout the mid to late 1990s.

In light of the various sources that explore skateboarder identity, this book is intended both as a development of existing ideas and the navigation of new territory. There are two main strands of discussion that run throughout this book. One examines the complex and varied nature of skateboarder identities and the ways in which girls and women have held and created space for themselves within sexist and hetero-masculine skateboarder identity narratives and practices. There are lots of different kinds of skateboarders who identify in a variety of different, varying, and sometimes contradictory ways. Women's and girls' involvement within this milieu have been – and continues to be – similarly complex, presenting alternative perspectives to the dominant narratives that appear so loudly and so persistently to be 'representative' of skateboarders.

The other strand within this book seeks to define some of the main aspects of skateboarding's physical culture: to explore the physical activity

Introduction 3

of skateboarding, the moving body, and the social-spatial frameworks of skateboarding practice as being embedded within gendered frameworks. This book analyses the ways we move, where we choose to practice, how we move in relation to one another, and how movement affects our thinking and feeling. This strand operates through analytical frameworks borrowed from the fields of dance and performance to open up a new realm of enquiry within skateboarding. One that has only recently begun to be explored by academics such as Åsa Bäckström and Sophie Friedel, whose work is discussed in Chapter 4, and by Hunter Fine.[20]

Methodology

This enquiry has been explored primarily from my own perspective as a skateboarder and my awareness of skateboarding sources of information and artefacts that have come from my immersion in skateboarding culture. These multiple sources include blog sites, tweets, Instagram videos and stories, media platforms, print publications, message boards, video content, and personal correspondence with friends who are skateboarders, journalists and industry professionals, alongside philosophical texts, peer-reviewed research articles, and academic books. I began skateboarding in 1998, in a town in the midlands of England. At that time, the most available skateboarding terrain for me and my friends were the kerbs and carparks of our town centre, and the occasional ledge spot or stair set. My nearest skatepark was Radlands, some 30 miles away, which is now a part of skateboarding history, having been one of the first indoor skateparks in the UK and host to regular national and international skateboarding competitions. Me and my friends would take the train to a nearby village which had a mini-ramp in the middle of a field, to Milton Keynes to skate the bus station, or to Birmingham to 'reclaim the city'; an organised take-over in which large groups of skateboarders would gather together to make anti-skateboarding byelaws impossible to enforce. No one skateboarder can claim to have access to all aspects of what is such a varied culture, or every piece of information that would be relevant to these discussions. My participation in skateboarding culture has also varied in depth and frequency over the past 22 years, as it tends to do. I have never been a sponsored or professional skateboarder – my participation has always been as a committed and passionate hobbyist. The enquiry explored within this book comes from my own experiences, observations, readings, and questions about skateboarding with the aim of answering a series of theoretical concerns around femininity's place, visibility, and practice-based presence within skateboarding, both in terms of identity and politics, physical culture, and common knowledge frameworks.

4   *Introduction*

My approach to exploring this enquiry has been through a combination of three methods:

1. Analysis of existing populist interviews conducted by journalists with skateboarders and corresponding commentary from skateboarders and journalists in response.
2. Analysis of primary research in the form of interviews, questionnaires, and field work observation conducted by myself with skateboarders and skateboarder-related participants.
3. Analysis of existing academic research.

Working primarily from existing interview data was beneficial because this extant material has been born out of skateboarding culture and, in the majority of cases, has not been initiated by me; the opinions and perspectives gleaned from these sources have not been led in any way by me as researcher. Skateboarding is a culture in which interviews with professional skateboarders are a common form of popular cultural text. For the most high-profile skateboarders, there are often multiple interviews in existence, many of which cover similar or related issues. It is possible to build up a robust understanding of a particular perspective through reading across different interview sources. It has also been necessary to augment some of this data with additional primary research in the form of interviews conducted face-to-face or through questionnaires provided to participants via email.

It has been necessary to use primary research methods more centrally in Chapter 4, which discusses the work of skateboarding charity, SkatePal. I have worked extensively with the charity since 2015, including participation in the building of a skatepark in Asira Al-Shamalyia in the north of the West Bank, involvement in coaching young people at this skatepark, observing the skatepark site, having informal conversations with local people, and conducting semi-structured interviews in Arabic and English with the help of an interpreter. Observations and informal conversations were documented through journal accounts, whilst interviews were audio recorded and transcribed. There are several academic and populist articles in existence that discuss the work of skateboarding charities in the Middle East, but few include comments or opinions from local participants. It has been central to my argument within Chapter 4 to frame and analyse the effects of the charity through the perceptions and opinions of local people about the expressive movement of skateboarding, as much as to understand the local cultural significance of sport, dance, and skateboarding and people's connections between them. Observations of skateboarders and skateboarding settings in a variety of cities and countries (and from my position as a skateboarder) has been the most pervasive method used within this research.

This enquiry has also drawn upon academic research on skateboarding across a variety of disciplines. By bringing together the cultural texts of skateboarding with primary research and existing theory, I have sought to present a rigorous study that recognises the connections to and gaps within existing theory and to arrive at new or developed understandings through a convergence of insights from these different research methods and knowledge sources.

Feminal

One of the terms used within this book is 'feminal', an archaic English word meaning 'relating to a woman'. This word seemed most appropriate for the overarching discussion and ideas within this book because of the fact that I have drawn upon a wide range of perspectives from different skateboarders who identify in a variety of ways. This book is not strictly or only 'about' women skateboarders; it is about the ways in which skateboarding culture relates to people who identify as women and girls, how skateboarding culture(s) are framed and understood in relation to gendered concepts (particularly femininity), and how we might re-examine skateboarding as being related to femininity as much as it may be related to masculinity. The term feminal was also chosen because of its differentiation from the word 'female'. In culture 'female' has strong connotations to hormonal and anatomical markers of womanhood that may not be considered inclusive of all women. Although the term 'female' as a 'biological' category is understood to be *as* socially produced as the terms 'woman' or 'women', this book looks at gender within skateboarding culture and does not venture into discussions about gender expression through physiological and hormonal processes. With this in mind, I have sought to use the more typical cultural term 'women' for consistency.

The idea of 'relating to' in the word feminal is also appropriate because of the ways that gender slips so easily between categories and is most often understood in relationship between gender identity expressions. For example, Chapter 1 uncovers the numerous monikers adopted by skateboarders who relate to femininity, including 'girl', 'woman', and 'witch', amongst others, each of which are formulated along a feminine gender spectrum and represent the desire to illuminate particular aspects of gender identity that other labels do not necessarily do justice to. In this way I have also sought to open up the field of enquiry along gender lines. Whilst feminine subjectivities are at the centre of this book, it is important to acknowledge how much my conception of the feminal is influenced by sources

6 *Introduction*

of knowledge and understanding created by non-binary and genderqueer theorists and skateboarders. This book particularly draws upon the experiences of skateboarders who currently (or have previously) self-identified as women. Throughout the book I have used the term 'women' within my own discussion, rather than 'womxn' or 'womyn', but I use the term to refer to all people who self-identify as women and whose identities incorporate feminine subjectivities. When referring to other people's writing, I have used the gender term the author expresses in their own writing. When referring to professional skateboarders who I do not have a personal connection with, I have reverted to pronouns widely used in popular discourse to refer to each individual, recognising that these may not be accurate, I have kept close watch of these skateboarders' self-authored Instagram and twitter accounts to try and ensure I am using each person's preferred pronouns within this text.

Girl as a radical state

The idea for this book came in part from my own experiences within skateboarding culture. It also came from research I conducted into 'girl' as a gendered concept, and from a desire to examine the embodiment of power and agency inherent within the 'girl' gender positionality. My enquiry focused around the impact and symbolism inherited from dominant – and it has to be acknowledged often Eurocentric – girl and related female-directed ideologies and archetypes. This work began with a consideration of the endurance and broad appeal of Alice from Lewis Carroll's 1865 novel, *Alice's Adventures in Wonderland*. Alice represents an iconic image of girlhood that originates from a European cultural context, but which has had a remarkable pervasiveness and appeal. Robert Philips asserts that '[b]y 1965, Alice's Adventures had been translated into forty-seven languages, including Latin, making it one of the world's most-translated books'.[21] Whilst Christoph Benjamin Schultz, writing in the catalogue from the Tate Liverpool gallery's 2011 exhibition on the influence of *Alice in Wonderland* on the visual arts, explains that *Alice's Adventures in Wonderland* has been 'consistently reissued and republished [such] that it has never been out of print'.[22] Given the endurance of Alice as a character, I was interested in the meanings associated with her. Alice is typically seen as a strong feminine archetype; she is rational, unperturbed in the strange environment of Wonderland and inquisitive, and she makes and trusts her own assessment of situations. Philosopher, Hélène Cixous describes Alice as 'unshakeable, powerful and full of authority'.[23]

When I began exploring Alice, this led me to another enduring female character, Shakespeare's Ophelia, who seems – at first – to contrast with Alice as a cultural symbol. Ophelia features in Shakespeare's play *Hamlet*

Introduction 7

and her narrative trajectory follows her demise as she is unable to cope with the death of her brother, to meet the demands of her father, or to cope with the mental deterioration of her lover, Hamlet. She eventually dies in a suspected suicide. Sinikka Aapola, Marnina Garrick, and Anita Harris chart the representation of Ophelia, referring to Mary Pipher's 1994 book named after her: *Reviving Ophelia: Saving the Selves of Adolescent Girls*, which presented an image of girlhood in crisis. They state,

> in the nineteenth century Ophelia was used to represent hysteria, which was at the time believed to be a real organic disease. … Hysteria became a major focus of scientific study with girls and women as its major target. … Ophelia also seems to symbolize the adolescent girl that the very influential educationalist and psychologist G. Stanley Hall established as the normative form of girlhood… adolescence was a turbulent and chaotic phase of life, and an archetypally feminine phenomenon.[24]

This association of female adolescence with hysteria extended well into the lives of adult women.[25]

Lesley Johnson has theorised this 'turbulence and chaos of girlhood' as representing the body in a state of radical openness. She refers to Russian philosopher Mikhail Bakhtin's reading of French Renaissance writer François Rabelais and his discussion of the 'grotesque body' that is frequently connected with the female. For example, in one passage the mouth and womb are related to Lucifer's gaping jaws, whilst in another he likens the grotesque body with the vagina.[26] Johnson writes, 'the grotesque body… is constantly growing, transgressing itself and its own limits… the image of the teenage girl as 'all arms and legs' intimated a bodily existence which was unfinished and open'.[27] Here Johnson rearticulates the adolescent female body as a powerful state of becoming – an unclosed and unfixed entity that poses a threat to the organising principles of patriarchal society in which femininity must meet narrowly defined standards.

The changes in body size Alice goes through in Wonderland place her body in this state of the unfinished, grotesque. Alice's girlhood is also associated with multiplicity and has been adopted to represent the multiple selves of the feminine by philosopher Luce Irigaray. In *Alice's Adventures in Wonderland*, Alice' cannot remember her name, and in trying to remember, thinks it begins with an L. Carolyn Burke explains,

> 'L' is, of course, multiple in Irigaray's reading: Alice, 'Alice,' Luce, and for a French speaker, elle/elles – the third person feminine, both singular and plural… elle(s) means to learn that the female self is multiple, that we are all written into the text.[28]

8 Introduction

Carroll's Alice is always already multiple in being a fictional character who was inspired by a real girl, Alice Liddell, the daughter of one of Carroll's colleagues. Although Irigaray's reading (as translated and described by Burke in the above quote) is centred on her interpretation from a French-language perspective, her insight highlights how the symbolic nature of language can serve to structure personal and social worlds. Through an understanding of the symbolic dimensions of the iconic and widely known European characters, Alice and of Ophelia, the metamorphosed and multiple body is symbolically aligned to a conception and image of femininity.

Johnson's articulation of girlhood as a 'powerful state of becoming' and these philosophical conceptions of girlhood refer to dominantly Western and European cultural readings, but they are echoed in Dwayne Dixon's research into youth within a Japanese context. Dixon discusses the appearance of the modern girl ('moga') in reference to a range of sources, highlighting the positionality of girls as 'between', occupying a space of challenge and peripherality. He writes,

> the girl-figure, composed from a panoply of discordant economic, familial, political, educational, and social forces, constitutes a [sic] entrancingly risky imaginary uncannily 'outside' of the normative, modernizing, patriarchal centripetal force exerted on the order of bodies and things. Girls are a facilitating function, imbued with powers to mother the nation even as, and precisely because, they are on its periphery.[29]

Dixon discusses how the non-normative position of girlhood comes about through the maternal potential of girls and their social status as both centred and peripheral.

Further to this, Jenny Nordberg writes about the cultural practices of 'Bacha Posh' in Afghanistan, where in response to the social pressure of having a male child (both as a sign of status and for practical purposes due to restrictions on women's movement and status outside the home) some families decide to dress their pre-pubescent daughters as boys. They do this to heighten family status, to enable the child to seek employment outside of the home and – in the rarer case of adult women Bacha Posh – they function as a form of intermediary between women and men, as a guardian (in the context of the hareem) and as escort.[30] Girlhood is – in this varying range of contexts – seen as a mutable form of gender construction. This book then comes in part from a desire to see gender categories expanded beyond an association between stereotypes and genitals, toward greater awareness of the spectrums through which each gender identity is elaborated. The multiple ways in which individuals do gender are expressed through these kinds

Introduction 9

of cultural stories that generate our conceptions of those gender categories, and the unconscious beliefs and biases that come with them.

In 2009, Eve Ensler, the author, playwright, and activist well known for her play *The Vagina Monologues* (1996), delivered a TED talk entitled 'Embrace Your Inner Girl'. In this, Ensler uses the metaphor of 'the girl cell' or group of cells to describe how gendered qualities typically associated with 'girl' have been devalued and at worst, eradicated, because they are seen as having no power or worth. She states:

> I want you to imagine that this girl cell is compassion, and it's empathy, and it's passion itself, and it's vulnerability, and it's openness, and it's intensity, and it's association, and it's relationship, and it's intuitive. And then let's think about how compassion informs wisdom, and that vulnerability is our greatest strength, and that emotions have inherent logic, which lead to radical appropriate saving action. And then let's remember that we've been taught the exact opposite by the powers that be. That compassion clouds your thinking, that it gets in the way. That vulnerability is weakness, that emotions are not to be trusted.[31]

For Ensler, the girl grouping of cells – or features typically associated with the broad gender category of girls – exist within all persons. Ensler's presentation encourages everyone to embrace and value these features as qualities of a balanced personhood and wider cultural ecology. This book echoes Ensler's desires for girls to be valued and for femininity in all forms to be embraced.

Throughout this book, I use both of the terms 'girl' and 'women' together ('girls and women') to denote people identifying broadly with a feminine gender spectrum in skateboarding. My use of both of these terms acknowledges the two most common monikers used by feminal participants and as a sign of respect toward the differing political connotations these words embody, which are discussed in Chapter 1.

Holden Caulfield

Skateboarding is said to have begun in the beach communities of California and its earliest conception involved basic manoeuvres on flat ground and gentle slopes, downhill racing, and the performance of freestyle tricks. The development of a dominant attitude and practice of skateboarding regarded as 'core', was heavily influenced by the pioneering activities of a team of surfer-skateboarders called the Zephyr Team (or the Z-Boys). In 2001, former Z-Boy Stacey Peralta directed the documentary *Dogtown and Z-Boys*, which tells the story of the Zephyr Team (est. 1973) and their contribution

10 *Introduction*

to the development of modern skateboarding practice through first-hand accounts from several members of the original team. As is documented in this film, skateboarders have from this early period, identified with a somewhat insular and counter-cultural identification.[32]

Skateboarders 'outsider' positionality is also recognised in the historic association of skateboarding culture to the J.D. Salinger novel *The Catcher in the Rye* (1951). In an interview with *Monster Children*, influential professional skateboarder Mark Gonzalez discusses how he was introduced to the book by Zephyr Team member Peralta in the 1980s. Gonzalez remembers him saying of the book, 'this is a classic. You gotta read this... this is the book you're gonna wanna read'.[33] J.D. Salinger's protagonist, Holden Caulfield, is an icon of teenage rebellion with contempt for the pretensions of social rules and adult authority. The image of the catcher in the rye that Caulfield keeps returning to in the novel represents a kind of perpetual child intent on ensuring other children don't fall off the cliff and into the realms of adulthood. The book was still circulating in my own skateboarding circles in the 1990s and 2000s, and I can remember people talking about it and recommending it to each other. Skateboarders delight in the enigmatic qualities of other skateboarders and scenes, which is perhaps most obviously identified in British skateboarding legend Tom Penny's cult status, which came about through his repeated disappearances from the scene during the 1990s and 2000s.[34] He is known for his quiet, thoughtful, and understated composure and, in one Penny myth, is said to have skated a competition in St. Albans in 1997 with a copy of *Catcher in the Rye* visible in his back pocket.[35]

Unconventionality and counter-cultural or outsider positioning have remained as popular themes with skateboarders throughout the decades, despite skateboarding's increased mainstreaming, as is discussed in Matthew Atencio, Becky Beal, E. Missy Wright, and ZáNean McClain's *Moving Boarders: Skateboarding and the Changing Landscape of Urban Youth Sports* (2018). In more recent years skateboarding's counter-cultural positionality has been most clearly recognised in the practices of women skateboarders. In a 2016 article titled, 'Why Women's Skateboarding is More Punk than Men's,' Sam Haddad argues that women's skateboarding is practised by relatively small but dedicated numbers with little recognition or financial backing such that women have persistently had to operate through DIY and self-supporting networks.[36] Relatedly, in an interview with professional skateboarder Sarah Meurle, Jan Kliewer and Tom Botwid state, '[i]n a time where skateboarding is so accepted and trendy I feel like female skaters are the only real underground skaters left, facing many of the obstacles older skaters still romanticise, like being an outcast, being different and/or underground etc.'.[37] At the same time, women are becoming increasingly central and supported within the peripheral outward-facing

Introduction 11

realm of competitive skateboarding, such as the X Games and Street League Skateboarding, particularly since the Women's Skateboarding Alliance headed a successful campaign for gender pay equality at the X Games, which became effective in 2008.

Skateboarding has changed considerably. Skateboarders from the 1960s, 1970s, 1980s, and beyond have, of course, all grown up. Many of them are married or in long-term partnerships and have children, work in typical jobs, and some run businesses. Many of the most influential skateboarders are now in their 40s, 50s, and 60s, and have accumulated life experiences that provide them with a markedly different perspective on the world than their adolescent former selves. This book seeks to unpack women's and girl's fight for recognition and inclusion at a time when skateboarding culture is showing increasing signs of a commitment to fostering supportive and inclusive spaces. As Thomas Barker, executive director for the International Association for Skateboard Companies tweeted,

> I love that where the energy is in skateboarding right now is in the groups that were traditionally left out of skateboarding. SB [skateboarding] at its heart is just punks that society has left behind channeling rage and creating community through a piece of wood.[38]

Barker's notion of a transference of energy illustrates what is seen by many in skateboarding as its current moment. With its emphasis on a DIY sensibility and with practitioners who embrace an activity that inherently trains participants in resilience, persistence, and community organising, skateboarding may have inadvertently set up the cultural conditions and social frameworks for feminal participants to create their own communities and to begin channelling their own rage.

Max Harrison-Caldwell's article examining what is meant by a 'core' of skateboarding, offers further insights into the dynamics operating between different skateboarder groups and ideas. He writes,

> the enforcement of a singular vision of core may in part be a reactionary response to [skateboarding's] new plurality. When people pushed to the margins of skate culture create their own popular tricks, dress codes, events, and publications, traditionalists fear that skateboarding isn't being represented correctly.[39]

Attempts to maintain a core identity elaborated through style, clothing, and attitude are a claiming of lands. Once differences of opinion over tricks, outfits, and artefacts are taken away it is, of course, as Harrison-Caldwell concludes, the physical act of riding a skateboard regularly and durationally

12 *Introduction*

that really constitute its 'core' participants. This book aims to examine precisely this – the physical activity of skateboarding – and to understand the ways in which gender politics inherited from mainstream culture permeate into the physical activity of riding a skateboard and the ways in which we understand and assert what it is we do. This book is for skateboarders, and particularly for anyone who has felt out of place on a skateboard, in a skatepark, or around other skateboarders.

Roots and routes

My own route into skateboarding was not initially through the physical practice. Whilst looking through the magazine racks at WHSmith's newsagent I came across *Sidewalk Surfer* magazine – a leading British skateboarding publication at that time. I was drawn to the image on the cover of a man mid-trick hovering above the ground. He had been photographed in the glow of a streetlight in an urban space empty of people. I saw that image as extremely seductive; it suggested magic, a sort of urban alchemy, and it represented an expansive freedom and open space. I bought the magazine and asked my parents for a skateboard for my 16th birthday along with a *411* video about 'How to Skateboard'. When the skateboard arrived, having little idea how to ride one, no friends to skate with, and living on the main road of a terraced house without a driveway or much concreted outdoor space, I positioned the skateboard statically on the carpet of my parent's front room and proceeded to learn to 'ollie'.

Eventually, I did find more appropriate places to skate and a group of friends to do it with, but it was not until much later that I became aware of the multifarious forms of movement held within the culture and the different sorts of communities that have developed. The organisation of this book is somewhat linked to my autobiography, beginning with two chapters that look at women's agency in skateboarding. In the first chapter, 'Girls and Women Holding and Creating Space in Skateboarding', I adopt a loose chronology of skateboarding from the 1960s to the present, to consider the ways in which girls and women have participated in skateboarding, and the cultural texts and social contexts that signify their status. In keeping with the conceptual understanding of 'girl', this chapter also looks at the ways in which the term 'girl' has been positioned in advertisements and skateboarding company representation. Chapter 2, 'Skateboarding and Feminism', offers a snapshot at the time of writing (2018–2019) of two of the most spotlighted feminal skateboarders and their self-formed conceptions of gender politics. This chapter looks in detail at numerous interviews conducted with Leo Baker[40] and Leticia Bufoni to highlight their shared and divergent political standpoints in relation to feminist theories.

Introduction 13

Chapters 3 and 4 focus on the physical activity of skateboarding and the symbolic, epistemological, and critical frameworks in which they sit. Chapter 3, 'Skateboarding Physical Culture' explores the institutional structures of body-knowledge that disassociate women and girls from 'bodily-kinaesthetic knowing'. This chapter examines the skateboarding learning process, the spaces in which skateboarding happens, and the emphasis in skateboarding on displays of 'struggle' that perpetuate a gender-based but not necessarily inherent hierarchy. Finally, Chapter 4, 'Skateboarding Philanthropy: A Somatic Practice Perspective' discusses skateboarding projects undertaken with disadvantaged communities and those experiencing war and protracted conflict as a gendered field of study. In this chapter I present an alternative approach through the consideration of a symbolic movement and somatic practice lens. This chapter uses as an exemplar the work of a UK-based charity: SkatePal – who build skateparks and teach children to skateboard in the Palestinian Territories, and with whom I have worked with as a volunteer, researcher, and ambassador since 2015. In particular, this chapter reflects on their Rosa skatepark project in a town in the north of the West Bank.

One of the points made within my final chapter focuses on how desires for movement differ from one person to another, as well as what you learn and understand through that movement. When I began to uncover alternative ways of moving on a skateboard, and seeing different sorts of bodies, including feminal ones, on skateboards, I became more aware of what it was that attracted me to this activity and how I wanted to move. Authentic expressions of movement are what I had been so drawn to initially and that attracted me to skateboarding culture, and what I have wanted to experience in my own body. Finally then, this book is also a call to express yourself through movement, to become more deeply connected to who you are – in whatever form that takes.

Notes

1 Jennifer Hargreaves and Eric Anderson, (2014), 'Sport, Gender and Sexuality: Surveying the Field' in J. Hargreaves and E. Anderson, (eds.), *Routledge Handbook of Sport, Gender, and Sexuality*, Routledge, London/New York, 3–18.
2 Judith Butler, (1990), *Gender Trouble*, Routledge, London/New York.
3 Kath Woodward, (2007), 'Embodied Identities: Boxing Masculinites' in I. Wellard, (ed.), *Rethinking Gender and Youth Sports*, Routledge, London/New York, 23–35.
4 Adele Pavlidis, (2012), 'From Riot Grrrls to Roller Derby? Exploring the Relations Between Gender, Music and Sport', *Leisure Studies*, 31(2), 165–176; Adele Pavlidis and Simone Fullager, (2012), 'Becoming Roller Derby Grrrls: Exploring the Gendered Play of Affect in Mediated Sport Cultures', *International Review for the Sociology of Sport*, 48(6), 673–688.

14 *Introduction*

5 Pavlidis, (2012), 169.
6 Carolyn Ali Khan, (2009), 'Go Play in Traffic: Skating, Gender and Urban Context', *Qualitative Inquiry*, 15(6), 1084–1102, 1091.
7 Paul O'Connor, (2020), 'Skateboarding as a Culture' in *Skateboarding and Religion*, Palgrave Macmillan, Cham, Switzerland, 9–12.
8 Becky Beal, (1996), 'Alternative Masculinity and Its Effects on Gender Relations in the Subculture of Skateboarding', *Journal of Sport Behaviour*, 19(3), 204–220; Alana Young, (2004), 'Being the Alternative in an Alternative Subculture: Gender Differences in the Experiences of Young Women and Men in Skateboarding and Snowboarding', *Avante*, 10(3), 69–82; Shauna Pomerantz, Dawn Currie, and Deirdre Kelly, (2004), 'Sk8er Girls: Skateboarders, Girlhood and Feminism in Motion', *Women's Studies International Forum*, 27, 547–557; Emily Chivers Yochim, (2010), *Skate Life: Re-imagining White Masculinity*, University of Michigan Press, Michigan; Åsa Bäckström, (2013), 'Gender Manoeuvring in Swedish Skateboarding: Negotiations of Femininities and the Hierarchical Gender Structure', *Young*, 21(1), 29–53.
9 Beal, (1996); Lia Karsten and Eva Pel, (2000), 'Skateboarders Exploring Urban Public Space: Ollies, Obstacles and Conflicts', *Journal of Housing and the Built Environment*, 15(4), 327–340; Yochim, (2010).
10 Lynda Johnston, (2016), 'Gender and Sexuality I: Genderqueer Geographies?', *Progress in Human Geography*, 40(5), 668–678, 669.
11 Stacey Peralta in Sean Mortimer, (2008), *Stalefish: Skateboard Culture from the Rejects Who Made It*, Chronicle Books, San Francisco, 23.
12 Michael Brooke, (1999), *The Concrete Wave: The History of Skateboarding*, Warwick Publishing, Toronto/Los Angeles.
13 Jocko Weyland, (2002), *The Answer Is Never: A Skateboarder's History of the World*, Century, London.
14 Sean Mortimer, (2008), *Stalefish: Skateboard Culture from the Rejects Who Made It*, Chronicle Books, San Francisco.
15 James Davis, (2004), *Skateboarding Is Not a Crime: Board Culture Past, Present & Future*, Carlton Books, London.
16 Patty Segovia and Rebecca Heller, (2007), *Skater Girl: A Girl's Guide to Skateboarding*, Ulysses Press, Berkeley, CA.
17 Natalie Porter, (2014), *The History of Women in Skateboarding*, Self-published.
18 Becky Beal, (2013), *Skateboarding: The Ultimate Guide*, Greenwood, Santa Barbara, CA; Becky Beal, (1995), 'Disqualifying the Official: An Exploration of Social Resistance in the Subculture of Skateboarding', *Sociology of Sport*, 12, 252–267; Beal, 1996.
19 Iain Borden, (2019), *Skateboarding and the City: A Complete History*, Bloomsbury, London; Iain Borden, (2001), *Skateboarding, Space and the City: Architecture and the Body*, Berg, New York.
20 Hunter H. Fine, (2018), *Surfing, Street Skateboarding, Performance and Space: On Board Motility*, Lexington Books, Washington, DC.
21 Robert Phillips, (1971), 'Foreword' in R. Phillips, (ed.), *Aspects of Alice: Lewis Carroll's Dreamchild as Seen Through the Critics' Looking-Glass 1865–1971*, Vanguard Press, New York, 15.
22 Christopher Benjamin Schultz, (2011), 'Down the Rabbit Hole and Into the Museum: Alice and the Visual Arts' in G. Delahunty and C.B. Schultz with assistance from E. Clayton, (eds.), *Alice in Wonderland Through the Visual Arts*, Tate Publishing, London, 18–19.

Introduction 15

23 Hélène Cixous, (1982), 'Introduction to Lewis Carroll's Through the Looking Glass and the Hunting of the Snark', Trans. M. Maclean, *New Literary History*, 13(2), 231–251, 237.

24 Sinikka Aapola, Marnina Garrick, and Anita Harris, (2005), *Young Femininity: Girlhood, Power and Social Change*, Palgrave Macmillan, Basingstoke/New York, 41.

25 Ibid.

26 Mikhail Bakhtin, (1968), *Rabelais and His World*, Trans. H. Iswolsky, The MIT Press, Cambridge, MA/London, 337–339.

27 Lesley Johnson, (1993), *The Modern Girl, Girlhood and Growing Up*, Open University Press, Buckingham/Philadelphia, 133.

28 Carolyn Burke, (1981), 'Irigaray Through the Looking Glass', *Feminist Studies*, 7(2), 288–306, 299.

29 Dwayne Dixon, (2014), 'Endless Question: Youth Becomings and the Anti-Crisis of Kids in Global Japan', PhD dissertation, Duke University. Available at dukespace.lib.duke.edu/dspace/handle/10161/8797 (Accessed 12 August 2019).

30 Jenny Nordberg, (2014), 'The Afghan Girls Raised as Boys', *The Guardian*, Sep 22. Available at https://www.theguardian.com/lifeandstyle/2014/sep/22/girls-boys-afghanistan-daughters-raised-as-sons-puberty-bacha-posh (Accessed 12 August 2019).

31 Ensler in TED 2010: n.p.

32 *Dogtown and Z-Boys*, (2001), Dir. Stacey Peralta, Sony Pictures, USA.

33 Mark Gonzalez in Goodfellow, Evan, (2015), 'Longform: Mark Gonzales', *Ride*. Available at https://www.monsterchildren.com/39710/longform-mark-gonzales/ (Accessed 2 October 2019).

34 Sidewalk, (n.d.), 'Tom Penny', *Sidewalk*. Available at https://sidewalkmag.com/people/tom-penny#sVhvEMluI6dVBcBg.97 (Accessed 9 October 2017).

35 Five Eyes Skateboarding, (2011), 'D.I.T.T. TOM PENNY (RARE) ST ALBANS 97 bonus section on GET OUT A Norwich skate video', *YouTube*. Available at https://www.youtube.com/watch?v=TiRKjKwkoOo (Accessed 9 October 2017).

36 Sam Haddad, (2016), 'Why Women's Skateboarding is More Punk than Men's', *Mpora*. Available at https://mpora.com/skateboarding/scene-stealers-womens-skateboarding-punk-mens#xLCUBQq1M0vx2hWR.97 (Accessed 10 October 2017).

37 Jan Kliewer and Tom Botwid, (2016), 'Sarah Meurle Interview & Part in Poetic Collective's "White Black Colour"', *Kingpin*. Available at https://kingpinmag.com/features/interviews/sarah-meurle-interview-part-poetic-collectives-white-black-colour.html#1uP0FCFlTBb3KCkz.97 (Accessed 10 October 2017).

38 Thomas Barker, (2019), Tweet, *Twitter*, May 7. Available at https://twitter.com/thomas__barker/status/1125636975027834881?s=20 (Accessed 12 August 2019).

39 Max Harrison-Caldwell, (2019), 'Let's Put This Shit to Bed', *Skateism*, May 31. Available at https://www.skateism.com/lets-put-this-shit-to-bed/ (Accessed 12 August 2019).

40 Leo Baker announced their change of name from Lacey Baker in late 2019 via social media channels.

1 Girls and women holding and creating space in skateboarding

One of the most enduring images still in existence depicting 1960s skateboarding culture is that of US champion Patti McGee[1] performing a handstand on a skateboard, which featured on the cover of *Life* (a US mainstream general interest magazine with a readership of millions during the 1960s)[2] in May 1965. In that same year she appeared on the US Mike Douglas show, showcasing some of her tricks and teaching Mike and two other guests to ride skateboards.[3] It was also the year that *Skater Dater* was released, a US-produced short film, written and directed by Noel Black. The coming-of-age story depicts a group of male skateboarders, one of whom keeps (literally) crashing into a girl in the neighbourhood who becomes his love interest. The boy begins spending time with the girl, to the dismay of his skateboarding friends. The end of the film sees the boy and the girl walking hand in hand down the street. The boy is no longer wearing the jacket and trousers of the rest of the skateboarding group; instead he has a smart shirt and jumper on symbolising his shift in attitude and his exiting from the 'childish' pursuit of skateboarding. The final scene shows the skateboarding group skate past two girls who look over at them with interest signalling their own potential 'coming of age'.[4] *Skater Dater* was the first film to feature skateboarding and skateboarders, it was released in the USA and won Best Short at the 1966 Cannes Film Festival. In 1968, it was released in the UK.

This chapter explores the ways in which girls and women have participated in skateboarding culture throughout its more than 50 years history, and how symbols of femininity and womanhood have been articulated and instrumentalised in relation to skateboarder identity. This chapter draws upon media forms across the decades, as well as interviews conducted with skateboarders from a range of sources.

Skater Dater was shot predominantly in Southern California and was well received at the time, according to Laura Thornhill Caswell, a former professional skateboarder who grew up in the area and whose career

Girls and women holding and creating space 17

with the Logan Earth Ski skateboard team ran from the mid to late 1970s. Remembering the film she explained,

> I'll never forget when I first saw [it]. It was a little dated cause it was made in the mid 60s. ... It was the coolest film, and this whole little romantic story that was going on was cute. Skateboarding had already progressed from what you saw in *Skater Dater*, to where it was [when I saw it] especially when the urethane wheel came out and with the advancement of trucks and boards, as it was really different to what was going on when *Skater Dater* was made... in a matter of 8 or 9 years the changes that had taken place were huge, but people loved that film. I think it turned on a whole wave of people to skateboarding and lit a fire under them.[5]

The freedom and agency of the all-male group flowing through the landscape was seen by Thornhill Caswell as an inspiration, albeit one that came with a somewhat 'corny'[6] storyline. In stark contrast to the centralisation of solely boy-group friendship, Thornhill Caswell remembers skateboarding in Southern California in the 1970s as a largely welcoming culture consisting mostly of boys who were happy to welcome girls into their crews and teams. Skateparks were spaces that demanded a high level of boldness and confidence in participants, which is very similar to the landscape of contemporary skateparks. She explains,

> At a skatepark you really had to be part of a line-up. ... You had to be there and participate and not just stand there like a wallflower. You had to own your space. I never felt unwelcome, as I was always encouraged. I never met with resistance or attitude from male skaters.[7]

From Thornhill Caswell's perspective in the 1970s, (heterosexual) relationships between skateboarders were considered an ideal scenario, enabling romantic partners to skate together and to appreciate each other's skateboarding practice. But as the narrative of *Skater Dater* suggests, boy and men skateboarders' involvement in relationships with girls and women who do not skate jeopardised their freedom to participate in skateboarding and signalled a skateboarder's adherence to mainstream normative culture. Lance Mountain, for example, has discussed how having a girlfriend was seen as restrictive in the 1980s. When he got married and had a child in his early 20s, he recounts how his sponsor Powell Peralta worried about whether they should keep his marriage under wraps for fear of it affecting sales.[8]

McGee was not a stand-alone champion in the 1960s, with several women competing in American National Skateboard Championships throughout the

18 *Girls and women holding and creating space*

1960s.[9] Similarly, Thornhill Caswell competed in the 1970s alongside regular girl competitors in Southern California including Robin Logan, Ellen O'Neal, Ellen Berryman, Edie Robertson, and others, which might suggest the growing interest of girls in skateboarding. Canadian short mockumentary directed by Claude Jutra, *The Devil's Toy*, produced in either 1966 or 1969 (there is some confusion[10]), pictures several girls taking part.[11] By the 1970s, women and girls are said to have numbered 25% of skateboarders in Southern California.[12] Though this is contested by Thornhill Caswell, who believes that numbers would have been much lower than that.[13] Similarly, in interviews with both Ellen Berryman and Kim Cespedes – professional contemporaries of Thornhill Caswell in the 1970s – they have commented on the few girls involved in skateboarding at the time.[14]

The 1970s culture of skateboarding in Southern California did seem to embrace girls' representation with their inclusion on skateboard teams alongside boys and with their images and interviews in magazines. Berryman also notes that her sister Cindy contributed written pieces to *Surfer* and *Skateboarder Magazine*.[15] Despite this, skateboarding in the 1970s was predominantly practised by boys and most commonly marketed at a base of boy and men practitioners. Most historical skateboarding publications refer to skateboarders using male pronouns, such as 'he', 'him', 'his',[16] and implicit in many publications aimed at skateboarders is that the reader identifies as a heterosexual man or boy. For example, in the 1978 edition of *Skateboard Annual* (published in London), the feature 'Board Talk', which is a glossary of skateboarding terms, includes a description of a 'catamaran' that explains, 'two riders skate sitting down on two boards and facing each other, with their legs and arms interlocked. Good manoeuvre to get to know that good looking girl rider'.[17] Within the relatively well-documented skateboard scenes of the UK, California, and Australia, female skateboarders did receive coverage with photographs in magazines, membership on skateboarding teams, and participation in professional competitions.[18] The absence of inclusive language exemplified in publications of the time highlight that despite their involvement female participants were not always recognised as a target audience for insider knowledge or as participants who shared the same cultural currency and belonging to the culture as boys and men did. Reflecting on this in 2019, female representation has increased considerably, but as Borden iterates in his most recent book about skateboarding, advertisements and team videos still emphasise an 'all-male camaraderie... that reinforces the notion that skateboarders are male, and that the absence of females is unproblematic'.[19]

Prior to the development of transition skateboarding (in backyard bowls and eventually on purpose-built ramps), which is usually credited to the pioneering skateboarding style of the Zephyr skate team (or Z-Boys) in the late

Girls and women holding and creating space 19

1970s,[20] popular skateboarding style in the late 1960s and 1970s involved the presentation of flatland tricks including pirouettes, handstands, kickturns, gliding, manual rolls, and other tricks that emphasised control, gracefulness, and flow, and which had a performance quality more akin to dance or ice skating. In her book discussing masculinity in relation to skateboard culture Emily Chivers Yochim suggests that this early style may have made skateboarding seem less 'contradictory' to women's involvement,[21] perhaps because it was more appealing to girls and women, or because it may have been seen as an appropriate form of physical activity for women and girls to perform.[22] Berryman, who skated for the Bahne team has a background in gymnastics and described her physical practice on a skateboard as being like performance art and dance. She says,

> What I really liked was the choreography aspect of the freestyle. There's not a lot of footage of that, because people weren't carrying around movie cameras and it was before video cameras. But we did freestyle routines to music and it was a kind of dance.[23]

As a member of Bahne, during the 1970s Berryman participated in competitions as well as in demonstrations of skateboarding, including an appearance on stage at a Jethro Tull concert.[24]

The historical account of skateboarding's development through the practice of the Z-Boys tends to underplay the impact of more mainstream or ordinary freestyle tricks on skateboarding's development. Having grown up in the Los Angeles area and having been skateboarding at the same time as the Z-Boys, Barbara Odanaka highlights the lack of attention paid to other skateboarding scenes in California as part of historical accounts. Talking about her experience of witnessing the Z-Boys for the first time at the 1975 Del Mar national skateboarding competition, she says,

> I remember them having an interesting style, sliding around. They did the other tricks as well – some of those freestyle tricks they make fun of in later interviews. It was very exciting, and I remember being happy to see there was a girl on the team, Peggy Oki. But I don't remember being part of a crowd that thought it was weird or that we didn't get it.[25]

Freestyle skateboarding has tended to occupy a derisory place within skateboarding culture. Borden suggests it has been pitched as 'skateboarding's feminine or homosexual "other" [with] its emphasis on grace and technique contrasting with the overt risk-taking of much transition and street skating'.[26] This has developed despite the fact that freestyle physical culture has contributed as much to skateboarding's development as the pool riding

20 *Girls and women holding and creating space*

Figure 1.1 Laura Thornhill Caswell, one-foot nose wheelie, 1976. Image by James Mahoney.

practices of the Z-Boys. Rodney Mullen, who began skateboarding in the mid 1970s and became a professional freestyle skateboarder in 1980 with the Bones Brigade is popularly credited with having invented most of the tricks that have become standard practice in skateboarding, including the flat-ground ollie, the kickflip, the heelflip, the 360-flip, and many more.

What is apparent about skateboarding throughout the 1960s and 1970s is the presence of mainstream, as well as more counter-cultural forms of skateboarding practice. Organised competitions began initially in 1963,[27] with professional teams that had coaches and in some cases choreographers. Skateboarders' use of the streets in the 1960s and 1970s however was often considered a nuisance, as can be seen depicted in the *Skater Dater* narrative, *The Devil's Toy*, and in *Dogtown and Z-Boys*. Thornhill Caswell discusses the ambiguous and multiple orientation of skateboarders in relation to authoritarians, explaining,

> [t]here was definitely an element of being a rebellious rule-breaker at times, but… I was going to all the new parks that were opening, I was

Girls and women holding and creating space 21

skating in contests and doing photo shoots... and starting to get paid. There were definitely only a small amount of people who were in that privileged position. Elsewhere there was... that more rebellious, skate-rat kind of lifestyle, constantly seeking out places to go skate where you weren't welcome to be. So you were always dodging the law and the authoritarians whose property you were trying to get on to. I dipped my hands a little bit in stuff like that.[28]

Thornhill Caswell's career extended across activities and contexts that represented both the legitimised and the outlawed character of skateboarding. In one story from this period she recounts how she was invited by the editor of *Skateboarder Magazine*, Warren Bolster, to travel with an assembled crew of skateboarders (all the rest of whom were boys) on a clandestine skate mission to the Arizona desert in search of a sea of hundreds of gigantic full-pipes that were yet to be installed as part of the Carter administration's strategy to supply water to drought-stricken towns and cities in the region.[29] Similarly, in an interview, she recounts an incident when she and some friends ditched school (in 7th grade) so that they could skate an empty back-yard pool. The police arrived and arrested the group on the more minor grounds of lack of adult supervision, as opposed to trespassing or playing truant.[30]

Figure 1.2 Laura Thornhill Caswell, full-pipe Arizona desert, 1976. Image by Warren Bolster

22 *Girls and women holding and creating space*

When skateboarding suffered its second major decline toward the end of the 1970s (the first was at the end of the 1960s and was due to the poor standard of equipment and subsequent injuries that ensued), it effectively lost its legitimisation as a 'sport' and professional career, but skateboarding's more delinquent thread continued and in the 1980s became a major theme and focus. Due to injuries, toward the end of the 1970s skateparks were becoming subject to increased insurance premiums that led to closures and the destruction of several parks.[31] With fewer skateparks and a lack of support for new entrants through the more sanctioned skateboarding arena, there were fewer participants, which led to the closure of shops and the folding of skateboard companies. Due to the lack of places to skate, skateboarders who continued to practice – particularly former members of the Z-Boys and the newly formed Bones Brigade (an all-men/boys team led by Stacey Peralta) – began building their own ramps in back gardens, sometimes organising their own festival-atmosphere events with participant-led 'competitions' that adopted a disorderly character.[32] Alongside this, throughout the 1980s street skateboarding continued to develop with skateboarders being forced into more regular interactions with police and security staff. Hunter H. Fine has charted skateboarding's shifting spatial legitimacy,[33] highlighting the ways that skateboarding's (often ambiguous) acceptance within and rejection from mainstream culture has led to its lack of integration into typical spatial zoning. He writes,

> There is no prescribed way to use a skateboard in the city except for not-at-all, as there are bicycle lanes for bicycles, sidewalks and crosswalks for pedestrians, roads and parking spaces for automobiles and ordinances, and restrictions that prohibit street-skating from all of these zones. The practice is not allowed in the everyday street for which it is designed, intentionally removed, it is a unique cultural gesture that is often out of place.[34]

The anxiety of skateboarding's impact – both physically on individual bodies and economically due to the liability of business owners – has led to a unique relationship between skateboarders and public space authorities, and the historical construction, destruction, and reconstruction of skateparks, running concurrently with the development of street skateboarding as a cultural practice that has been seen as many things: an innocent street activity, a dangerous street activity, a vague annoyance to the dominant users of the streets, as nuisance, as vandalism, and as a form of civil disobedience. Skateboarding's shifting status in relation to mainstream culture became distinctively connected to this last point in the 1980s. As Porter explains, 'if

Girls and women holding and creating space   23

you wanted to skate you had to take on a rebellious, outlaw attitude because that's what society was saying skateboarding was'.[35]

Becky Beal refers to 1980s skateboarding culture as 'lean times for women'.[36] Cara-Beth Burnside, who was born in California in 1968 and began skateboarding in the late 1970s, discusses the period of the late 1980s and early 1990s explaining, 'It was really hard and intimidating as the only girl out there. ... There was definitely a vibe of feeling out of place. Certain guys would look at you like you were an alien or something'.[37] Despite being attracted to skateboarding as a 'rebel sport', Burnside explains that during the 1980s there were no women's or girl's contests that she could participate in.[38] She became a professional snowboarder as a way to make money that could enable her to continue to participate in skateboarding.[39] She describes skateboarding in amateur contests alongside guys, and in 1989 she was the first woman to feature on the cover of *Thrasher* magazine.

Skateboarding at this time is often discussed through its association with punk rock, drawing on a symbolic connection between subcultures that emphasised an anti-authoritarian and anti-mainstream ethos, aggressive and confrontational attitudinal tropes, and a commitment to shared subcultural values that foregrounded participant authenticity (and therefore the need to stratify participants on the basis of their commitment and authenticity). Michael Brooke – publisher of *Concrete Wave* magazine – is quoted in an article published in *Huck* Magazine explaining that punk rock appealed to both male and female skateboarders but that it made the skateboarding industry as a whole more testosterone driven.[40]

Although the 1960s and 1970s showed much promise for an equitable skateboarding arena inclusive of women and men, the decline of skateparks and the extant industry at the end of the 1970s precipitated a shift that dramatically decreased the number of women participants and led skateboarders to re-forge their activity in a way that was less likely to appeal to or be welcoming of a broad participant group. That said, both ramp and street practice as they developed in the 1980s and beyond were heavily influenced by the pioneers of skateboarding in the 1960s and 1970s, particularly freestyle, and many of these practitioners and pioneers were women.

Insiders

From the earliest waves of skateboarding female skateboarders have held space within core, typically men-dominated skateboarding arenas and found ways of carving out space for themselves. This continued throughout the difficult 1980s. For example, during the mid to late 1980s Bonnie Blouin regularly wrote articles for the 'Skater's Edge' feature in *Thrasher* magazine. Her articles were focused on skateboard culture generally including

24 *Girls and women holding and creating space*

discussions about skate sticker collecting,[41] the nuisance of pedestrians,[42] and skateboarders getting older.[43] Lynn Kramer began the *Equal Time* zine in 1988, which featured North American women skateboarders. In 1989, Laura Medlock formed the Women's Skateboard Network, which according to Patty Segovia and Rebecca Heller 'consisted of more than 250 girls in five countries'.[44] In the same decade, around 1983 or 1984, the women-oriented punk skateboard club, 'The Hags', was formed by Sevie Bates – a group of around ten that skated and partied together in Los Angeles and who were influenced by the Z-Boys and a San Francisco-based men-dominated skate crew called 'The Jaks'.[45] In an interview with Emily Savage for *BUST* Magazine, Bates explains 'I remember telling Tony [Alva], "I should be in the Jaks, because I can skate better than a lot of these guys. … It pissed me off. It was a dude thing, like a motorcycle club".'[46] In response to her exclusion, Bates formed 'The Hags' which one former member described as a 'feminist statement'.[47]

The 2018 film *Skate Kitchen* (Dir. Crystal Moselle), illustrates the lingering need for women's camaraderie and space-making. The film follows a fictional narrative but with elements of documentary as it draws on the lives of an extant collective of New York City skateboarders who call themselves 'Skate Kitchen'. The group is women-dominated and the film reflects on some of the gendered social difficulties experienced by the group, in particular their fraught relationship with a local all-men crew. One of the tensions that comes up in the narrative is lead-character Camille's integration with the all-men crew. Although the narrative is at times overly dichotomous (particularly in the separation of women and men in their respective groups) and in this way is not 'true to life',[48] Moselle captures Camille's desire for recognition and acceptance by the all-men group in a way that delicately reflects on the hegemonic gender dynamics of skateboarding in which being 'one of the guys' is considered the highest form of approval.[49]

Alongside these accounts and perspectives, there is also some evidence of support and encouragement for female skateboarders in skateboarding publications. In two editions during 1987 and 1988, *Transworld Skateboarding* magazine ran an advertisement from the Powell Peralta skateboard company featuring Leaf Trienen and Anita Tessensohn, which included the text, 'Some Girls Play with Dolls. Real Women Skate'.[50] The advert is interesting firstly in its support of women skateboarders, and particularly at a time when skateboarding is perceived to have been at its most aggressive, masculine, and unfriendly toward women. It is also interesting to see the distinction made between the terms 'girl' and 'woman' that reflects feminist discourse of the time.

Historically the term 'girl' has been used to describe the gender-age category of a young woman, alongside a varied range of other connotations

Girls and women holding and creating space 25

depending on the context and manner in which it is positioned.[51] As Maddie Crum points out in her interview with Sally McConnell-Ginet, infantilising words – such as 'child', 'girl', and 'boy' – have been used as a means to diminish a person's status particularly for Black women and men within an American colonial context.[52] Second-wave feminists insisted on avoiding the term 'girl' precisely because of its derogatory use as applied to women.[53] Instead, the terms 'woman' and 'young woman' were adopted 'as signifiers of seriousness, equal standing, and adult or mature status'.[54] Within a Western context, 'girl-ness' or what it is to be a girl, has moved through a process of reclaiming alongside the political context of post-feminism. A movement frequently cited as part of this reclaiming is that of the 'Riot Grrrls', which is commonly thought to have developed from the feminist politics of female punk musicians during the 1990s. In fact, the history of 'girl' empowerment actually originates from young African American women in the 1980s.[55]

Owning sexualisation

The popular British pop group The Spice Girls are often referred to in discussions of 'girl power' for their explicit references to feminist politics alongside the reclaiming of the 'girl' label within a UK mainstream and commercial context. The Spice Girls' playful presentation of five female types fed directly into narrow and at times offensive and exclusionary cultural stereotypes.[56] They presented a safe and sellable version of feminism that only partially challenged the cultural frameworks within which they were located but, as Catherine Driscoll has argued, 'there is something productive about girls acting on the world in ways that are widely accessible to the everyday lives of their audience'.[57] They may not have been doing 'feminism' in a way that pleased all feminists, but they were certainly exhibiting a great deal of freedom in doing and playing their own versions of 'girl' in a fun, highly central, visible, and popular way by performing, and ostensibly 'owning', their sexualisation.

The objectification of women as a facet of skateboarder identity increased in the 1990s, in a different way to the self-owned objectification adopted by some feminists, with a range of skateboard companies producing explicit sexual imagery of women on skateboard decks and in adverts. One of the most notable of which was the World Industries 'Randy Colvin' deck, designed by artist Marc McKee in 1991. The graphic, inspired by a centrefold published in the pornographic magazine *Penthouse* (1990), features a full-frontal nude depiction of a woman masturbating.[58] It is relevant to mention the contradictory existence of both sexualisation and support of women that is apparent in skateboard culture. Whilst World Industries

26   *Girls and women holding and creating space*

(and other companies) created content of this kind that explicitly sexualised women, they were also the first company to sponsor a woman street skater in 1991 – Saecha Clark.[59]

This sort of compartmentalisation allows for multiple competing and apparently conflicting practices and approaches to sit within the same culture for different purposes. For example, the sexualisation of women in skateboarding graphics and adverts serves the purpose of defining a dominant sexuality through hetero-masculine pornographic material alongside sometimes misogynist graphic content. The use of sexualised and graphic content was also instrumental as a way of presenting a counter-mainstream and deliberately anti-social cultural stance. As Borden notes,

> *Big Brother* magazine explicitly attacked the apparently cosy attitudes of manufacturers, magazines and skateboarders. One tactic involved printing explicitly sexist articles, photographs, and advertisements. For example, one issue contained readers' letters describing themselves as a 'pussy getting machine,' an advertisement for the 'fuct' company with women spanking each other with skateboards, another for 'hooters' skateboard wheels with breast and nipple graphics and the slogan 'urethane for men' and an article on 'how to pick up girls.'[60]

A side effect of this cultural stance was the positioning of women and homosexual skateboarders outside of core skateboarder identity. For homophobic and misogynist core skateboarders, this may have been a desired effect.[61]

It is important to put *Big Brother* into a cultural and geographic context as only one of many skateboarding publications in existence. Vintageskat eboardmagazines.com discusses the magazine's popularity in somewhat contradictory ways. The site explains that

> Love it or loathe it everyone read it. … Content was highly controversial and no subject was taboo, as well as skating there was a lot of sex, nudity, drugs and rock n roll not to mention religion and midgets. Articles such as 'how to kill yourself' in No3 and 'field trip to Hustler' in No9 gained the magazine 'outraged' media exposure and a spot on several news broadcasts. Despite all of this the mag was instrumental in publishing video sequences of the newest tricks and covered many rising street skaters.[62]

Despite the suggestion that the magazine was extremely popular ('everyone read it'), the site also states that it was never financially viable and lacked distribution, remarking 'it only ever ran to monthly print runs of

Girls and women holding and creating space 27

20,000 to 30,000'.[63] The controversial nature of *Big Brother* has led to its legendary status and a perhaps over-inflated sense of its centrality in skateboard culture (particularly outside the USA), but it does highlight the ways in which core skateboarding culture has historically used women as a way of elaborating a dominant White, male (USA-based), and hetero-sexual agency.

Critical awareness

Signs of critical self-awareness around the objectification of women are apparent in other sources. For example, the 1990s also saw the creation of skateboard company Girl in 1993 by professional skateboarders Mike Carroll and Rick Howard alongside Spike Jonze and Megan Baltimore. Jonze and Baltimore worked for World Industries where Carroll and Howard were team riders for subsidiary company, Plan B. The story behind the name 'Girl Skateboards' is depicted in a video celebrating 20 years of the company. Shot in the style of an old silent movie, the video shows Carroll and Howard sat in a diner in Torrence, CA, trying to come up with a name for their new company. In the film, Carroll suggests a series of possible names by writing them out on a pad of A4 lined paper, which he holds up and presents across the table to Howard. Each one is disregarded by Howard as 'lame'. Carroll's final attempt to impress comes in the form of a cartoon drawing of a woman sat naked with her legs apart, baring her breasts and a hairy vagina. Howard responds with a look of tired disappointment. He gets up to go to the toilet, finds the men's cubicle locked and makes his way to the women's cubicle where he comes face to face with the toilet symbol for 'woman' (circle for a head and a simple body drawing of two arms, a skirt and two legs). In the film we see a shot of Howard's face expressing a look that says, 'I've got it'. The final shot of the film shows Howard and Carroll high-five and congratulate each other as they skate away past the diner.[64]

This narrative articulates a tongue-in-cheek humour around the sexuali-sation and objectification of women in board graphics and advertisements. The company name functions as a comment upon skateboarding compa-nies' enthusiasm for objectifying the female body in skateboard graphics, but by using the de-humanised toilet cubicle symbol for 'women' (or 'girl') rather than a pornographic image, Carroll and Howard are also making a knowing and ironically humorous statement at the same time. It's not clear how much this narrative was widely picked up by skateboarders at the time the company came into being, but it certainly reveals a capacity for critical self-reflexive engagement with skateboarding culture that may have raised questions – for individual skaters – about the sex-gender tropes operating

28 *Girls and women holding and creating space*

within the culture. The Girl skateboard company never sponsored a woman rider, but the company was progressive in having a woman co-founder, Megan Baltimore, who was regarded as the company 'matriarch'.[65]

Within this gendered political context, the 1990s was a decade that saw increased entrance of female skateboarders into the hallowed street skateboarding realm, including Jaime Reyes and Elissa Steamer amongst others, many of whom were documented in Lynn Kramer's zine *Equal Time*. Steamer debuted into world-wide skate culture on Toy Machine's 1996 *Welcome to Hell* video. Steamer's recognition is widely celebrated within skateboarding, but the prominence afforded to her was not extended to many of her contemporaries. I have argued previously that Steamer and many of her contemporaries elaborated a particular approach to skateboarding wherein the combination of outstanding skill and the performance of style that drew from typically masculine physical and social culture served as a form of social mobility enabling their acceptance within the core.[66] This is particularly interesting when, as Porter documents, in the 1970s competitive skateboarding circuit Ellen O'Neal was 'advised to avoid more masculine moves... which she promptly ignored'.[67] It is relevant to recognise here the different and shifting ways in which women's and girl's bodies are explicitly and subtly 'authorised' to partake in skateboarding physical culture from one decade to another.

It is also important to recognise how racial and gender politics intersect with skateboarding culture. In an interview published in *Jenkem*, Jilleen Liao has suggested that Hawaii-born Jaime Reyes has been overlooked within skateboarding culture as a result of systematic and inherent racism. She writes, '[a]lthough skateboarding is becoming more visibly intersectional, and more female skaters are rising to prominence (thanks in part to the democratizing power of Instagram), Jaime's name has been curiously left out of the discussion, almost to the point of erasure'.[68]

Throughout the 2000s, it was typical to see companies sponsor female skateboarders in a separate girls' division. This was not a blanket practice, but was typical in many cases.[69] The standard of skateboarding exhibited by the best women skateboarders is generally not matched with that of the best men and in this sense it has not been considered inherently bad practice to separate teams by gender (putting aside for a moment issues of gender dichotomy, which are a larger issue across the competitive and sporting arena). However, criticism has been levelled at the way women in female divisions are marketed and the fact that women's teams (and individual female skaters) receive such limited exposure.[70] Skateboarder and writer, Anthony Pappalardo, has argued that women skateboarders tend to be held to higher and more technically adept standards than men skateboarders in order to prove themselves.[71]

Girls and women holding and creating space 29

In competitions, women skateboarders have had to campaign for plat-forming and equal prize money. In 2002, Burnside, Mimi Knoop, and Jen O'Brien convinced ESPN to host a girl's demo at the X Games, which developed into their first women's vert event in 2003.[72] In 2005, Burnside, Knoop, and Drew Mearns founded Women's Skateboarding Alliance to support women's participation within the skateboarding competitive and professional industry. Through discussion with ESPN executives, they successfully secured a rise in prize money for women at the 2006 X Games, and eventually achieved equal prize money in 2008.[73] Despite these considerable gains in respect and value of women's participation, there are still large divisions in prize money between women and men. In 2015, Leticia Bufoni won the Street League Skateboarding Nike SB Super Crown women's division (the first time a women's division was included) claiming $30,000 in prize money (plus a watch worth $11,000). The men's contest was won by Kelvin Hoefler, who in contrast claimed $200,000.[74]

A major problem in the separation of teams is the lower echelon status that is applied to women's skateboarding as a broad category. Skating 'like a girl' and being 'good for a girl' have become shorthand for a range of negative connotations associated with women's participation and feminine gender expression. In response to this, brands aimed specifically at supporting women skaters have arisen – mostly founded or run by women-identifying skaters. For example, taking aim specifically at the idea that girls are undervalued and that the word 'girl' is used in a derogatory way, 1970s professional vert skateboarder Cindy Whitehead founded the brand and website Girl is NOT a 4 Letter Word in 2013. In some English language colloquial contexts, the phrase 'four-letter word', is used as a stand-in for profane or swear words, which often – but not always – consist of four letters, such as 'shit', 'fuck', etcetera. Whitehead sells branded skateboard decks and clothing, documents the latest in news relating to female skateboarders, and administers micro-grants that enable women skateboarders and crews to apply for funding for travel, and to put on events. North American Silly Girl Skateboards (founded by Jamie Parker and Matt Gaudio in 2005), British Rogue Skateboards company (started by Jenna Selby in 2008), North American Hoopla Skateboards (founded by Mimi Knoop and Cara-Beth Burnside in 2013), and North American Meow Skateboards (founded by Lisa Whitaker in 2013) are brands that each have a central team made up entirely of girls. German Cheers Skateboards (founded by Sabrina Göggel in 2011) focuses on women skateboarders, but sponsors women and men within the team. The separation of a men's and women's roster has changed over the last five to ten years, with more companies constructing teams on the basis of a shared ethos rather than technical ability. For example, Welcome Skateboards (est. 2010) state on their website, 'we believe a

30 *Girls and women holding and creating space*

skateboard team should not be a collection of the skateboarders who are statistically or technically the best, but a family of individuals that get you excited to ride your skateboard'.[75] There are also several skateboard companies now who have one central team comprised of both male and female riders.

The broad landscape of skateboarding increasingly shows a heightened level of political awareness and a desire to develop knowledge and understanding of a range of issues, including those relating to womens' and girls' empowerment and equal standing. British brand Lovenskate has created what appears to be a contemporary re-fashioning of the Powell Peralta slogan 'Some Girls Play with Dolls. Real Women Skate', with their decks and t-shirts that read, 'Real Girls Skate Curbs'. The Lovenskate brand was started in 2001 by British skateboarder, Stuart Smith. Lovenskate sponsor a woman skateboarder on the team – Lucy Adams – who became pro for them in August 2017. Adams has been photographed and filmed wearing and showing support for the meanings associated with 'Real Girls Skate Curbs'.

Though there is no documentation discussing Lovenskate's decision to market the phrase, it signifies a reclaiming of the 'girl' label in a

Figure 1.3 Lucy Adams, switch front shuv, wearing 'real girls skate curbs' Lovenskate t-shirt, 2015. Image by Chris Johnson.

Girls and women holding and creating space 31

contemporary context, and furthermore associates girls with the underground, rebellious, and aggressive symbolism of the streets. Within skateboarding culture, curbs (or kerbs) are the most common and basic obstacles to skate. Most cities in the world delineate roads from pavement using kerb stones in at least some places, and they are usually set at a reasonably low height from the ground which allows beginners to develop skills in sliding and grinding tricks. Despite their status as 'basic' obstacles, kerbs are not denigrated as solely beginners' terrain; skating kerbs is often regarded as a way of going back to the roots of street-skating; they are emblematic of the basic freedom of street-skating and are the most prevalent form of street obstacle available to skaters.

Further to this, Smith has expressed an interest in centring female empowerment in his production of the Lovenskate 'Devrim Zamani' board (meaning 'Revolution Now' in Kurdish). The board features a female Kurdish freedom fighter with an image of a butterfly in the foreground. Smith recounts – in an interview with *Sidewalk* magazine – his decision to create the graphic, which was based on a chance encounter with the Kurdish owner of a mini-market in East London, who was sat reading a supplement from a Kurdish language newspaper. Smith explains,

> On the front page was one big photograph of a very pretty girl holding a rocket launcher with a whole load of other pictures of women dressed in camo gear holding AK47s. It was a really striking image. … On the back of the supplement was a picture of butterflies in the countryside. The juxtaposition struck me so I asked the guy what it was about. He went on to explain that it was an article about female freedom fighters up in the Kurdish controlled Syrian mountains who are part of something called the 'YPG' in Kurdish and the 'People's Protection Units' in English. … I went home and read a little bit more about it. … I love the idea that in a part of the world where gender roles are much more stringently applied than in the West, that this feminist group had taken it upon themselves to protect the Kurdish people.[76]

In stark contrast with the kind of sexualised graphics featuring women during the 1980s and 1990s (and in the present), the Devrim Zamani board highlights a progressive, politically aware strand of feminal interest and support. Rather than representing a stereotypical connection of fragile beauty symbolised between the girl and the butterfly, the butterfly has a meaningful alignment to Smith's initial encounter with the shopkeeper, which makes a visual and thematic (rather than simplified gender symbolic) connection between the freedom fighter girl and the sense of freedom and beauty encapsulated in the image of a butterfly.

32 *Girls and women holding and creating space*

Figure 1.4 Lovenskate Devrim Zamani deck, 2015. Image by Nick Sharratt.

Girl-made communities

As a continuation of the space-making girls and women have initiated in skateboarding, Girl Skate Alliance and Girl is NOT a 4 Letter Word are two of several organisations founded by women who began skateboarding in the 1970s, 1980s, and 1990s, that support women skateboarders. For example, Lisa Whitaker, a skateboarder since 1985 founded Girl Skate Network in 2003, an online community and media platform that documents women and girl skateboarders across the world. She also founded the Meow brand in 2012, which sponsors women riders. In an interview with Broadly (Vice), Whitaker explains that her decision to found Meow came about in response to the fact that 'most of the top girls in the world weren't sponsored and were not getting any media support'.[77] Similarly, Kim Woozy recognised the need for women in skateboarding to be given a platform and visibility so that they might inspire other girls and women to take part; in 2010, Woozy founded Mahfia – an Internet TV channel that documents and archives female skate crews and scenes from all over the world. Similarly, In the UK, former sponsored skateboarder and founder of Rogue Skateboards, Jenna Selby, has documented women's skateboarding since the early 2000s (she

Girls and women holding and creating space 33

started skateboarding in the 1990s). Selby has had her skateboard photography featured on numerous platforms, in 2009 she released the first UK and European all-women skateboarding film *As If, And What?*, she organises the women's competition at the National Action Sports Show (NASS) festival every year, and she continues to visit skateparks and spots primarily within the UK but also overseas, to document diverse women and gender non-binary riders.

In a TEDx talk Woozy included a quote originating from African American civil rights activist Marian Wright Edelman, 'It's hard to be what you can't see',[78] recognising that women and girls need to be exposed to role models that look like themselves in order to realise their involvement and potential within the skateboarding industry. This includes women taking part in skateboarding as well as taking up roles as writers, photographers, videographers, and competition judges, and to be seen contributing throughout the industry. In 2017, the diversity skateboarding magazine *Skateism* began worldwide distribution, after five years as an online magazine (founded by Moch Simos in 2012). Its remit serves to be a platform for alternative skateboarding cultures and alternative role models. *Skateism* documents LGBTQ+, women's, and global skateboarding scenes, and has

Figure 1.5 Teigan Komaromi, street plant, 2019. Image by Jenna Selby.

34 *Girls and women holding and creating space*

included features with trans woman skateboarder Cher Strauberry, Sandy Alibo's work with Surf Ghana (a collective of skateboarders, surfers, and creatives), and Annie Dean-Ganek's production of a short documentary *Carving Space*, which makes visible and discusses queer skateboarding culture.

Within skateboarding communities across the world and particularly in the USA, Canada, the UK, and Australia, 'girl' identification has been wholeheartedly taken up by a range of skaters, skate crews, teams, and organisations, Including Girl Skate UK, Girl Skate India, Skate Like A Girl, Girl Skate Australia, Girl Riders Org, and Skate Girls Tribe amongst others. These groups and organisations are often focused around collective support and experiential exchange. Atita Verghese co-founded Girl Skate India in 2015 to teach girls to skate and to promote gender equality. Verghese also organises skate tours for women and gender non-binary skaters from all over the world, which bring together different people to skate cities in India and to meet local skateboarding communities of girls and women.

There are also groups that do not refer to themselves as 'girls' but through some other moniker – women, womxn, gals, witches, babes, and so on. For example, Canadian skateboarder, Stephanie Battieste founded the 'Babe's Brigade' in 2015 as a supportive community for women skateboarders, and a brand. Battieste organises skateboarding events and runs lessons for girls and women, recognising the varied ways that female skateboarders identify and connect with skateboarding culture and that there is a need for girls and women to explore and connect with an expression of self to gain self-confidence. She says, 'I'm trying to find a way that I can give a very authentic look into the lives of… who these women are as skaters. … I think that confidence kinda has to do with an understanding of oneself'.[79]

Engaging critically with the female or girl label, Kristin Ebeling and Shari White's *Skate Witches Zine* documents 'non-traditional' skateboarders, many of whom identify as women or girls, but Ebeling – at least – refuses the label 'female', whilst the name 'skate witches' comes from a 1986 satirical short film directed by Danny Plotnick about three female skatepunks who terrorise boy skaters.[80] Ebeling states,

> I'm a female skateboarder, but unfortunately, I can't say that with any authentic sense of pride. This is not because I don't identify as female, or because I'm not a feminist. I am… it's because being known as "the girl skateboarder" since I was 12 years old has been more or less a terrible experience.[81]

During the 2019 Pushing Boarders skateboarding conference, Ebeling featured on 'The Revolution Will Not Be Patronised' panel during which she

Girls and women holding and creating space 35

talked about her determination not to use the word 'female' to avoid alienating transwomen, intersex women, and others who do not necessarily meet the biological connotations associated with being 'female'.

There are many different ways to be a girl, and the word is increasingly used within populist discourse and academic discussions of gender culture as a symbol for characteristics and behaviour that are not – or not only – exhibited by 'young' women. Jennifer Baumgardner and Amy Richards articulate this in their discussion of what it is to 'be a girl'. They write,

> [d]o we mean those preadolescents who are climbing trees and playing with Barbie? Or do we mean those grown women on *Sex in the City* who in their independence, their bonds with female friends, and their love of feminine fashion invoke a sense of eternal girlhood? We mean both.[82]

The qualities implied in Baumgardner and Richards's examples can be summarised as playfulness, physical confidence, independence, and interrelational communication and support, alongside a confidence in expressing an avowedly 'feminine' appearance. 'Girl', then, can be understood as a form of gender expression not limited to any particular sex classification, and importantly, not limited to people in a particular age category or either.

Finnish woman, Lena Salmi, took up skateboarding at the age of 61. Her entry point was longboarding, which she began at aged 57 as a form of transport.[83] Salmi administrates a Facebook group titled 'Very Old Skateboarders and Longboarders', which supports others who are 'older than normal' skaters, 'who may have been told "you're too old for doing that" but don't care'.[84] A Time Out video documenting the group includes two other older women riders from London – Sabina Edwards (aged 56 in the video) and Elizabeth (aged 66 in the video), who are also members of the group. They describe people's awe and derision at seeing elder women on a skateboard. Elizabeth explains how two people stopped her while she was skateboarding saying, 'I'm so sorry to stop you, but I thought I was having a hallucination'.[85] The Facebook group has more than 4000 members (of a variety of ages) and though it is still relatively rare to see someone in their 50s or 60s riding a skateboard, the group is not the only one of its kind aimed at 'older than average' skateboarders.

California-based 'Skateboard Moms and the Sisters of Shred' is a community platform on Facebook started by Barbara Odanaka. In her mid 30s and struggling with the pressures of becoming a new mother, Odanaka sought the help of a therapist who encouraged her to do something she used to enjoy as a child for ten minutes everyday. Having begun skateboarding

36 *Girls and women holding and creating space*

in 1971, getting back on a board was the first thing that came to her mind and she describes the experience as liberating and uplifting. She explains,

> the moment I put my foot on the skateboard, it was like going back in time and I felt that same sensation, that joy. Really, just literally putting my foot on the board and taking the first push. It was so liberating, and my spirits were lifted, and all those other clichés came true. It was like being 10-years-old all over again.[86]

In 2016, Odanaka was 54 years old, still skateboarding and supporting other women – not necessarily moms – mostly in their 30s, 40s, and 50s to start skateboarding or to rekindle a childhood interest in skateboarding.

Conclusion

No culture exists in a vacuum and skateboarding 'corresponds'[87] to the mainstream politics of different eras within specific geographic and globalised contexts. The earliest wave of skateboarding's popularity from the mid 1960s and throughout the 1970s has been memorialised particularly through the activities of the Z-Boys as an outsider pursuit, and elaborated through shows of aggressive localism and anti-social behaviour despite its initial popularity and organisation as a sport, dance form, and leisure practice. In the documentary, *Dogtown and Z-Boys*, the narrative describes how the group of local surfers who formed the Zephyr surf team had developed an aggressive localism. At that time, the group had colonised 'the Cove', amidst the derelict pier of Pacific Ocean Park, and would spray-paint the area with statements like 'go home' directed at outsiders coming there to surf. During the film members of the Zephyr Team talk openly about throwing debris from the pier at unknown surfers in the water.[88]

Hanson O'Haver has argued that skateboarding's early development came at a time of paranoic libertarianism in US politics, which was defined by insularity and a desire for personal freedoms over state regulation. He writes,

> It's not insignificant that the first independent U.S. skateboarding magazine, *The Quarterly Skateboarder* (later *Skateboarder Magazine*), was published in 1964, the same year that saw Barry Goldwater's landmark Republican nomination, as well as the publication of Richard Hofstadter's infamous *Harper's* essay, 'The Paranoid Style in American Politics,' which maligned the 'heated exaggeration, suspiciousness, and conspiratorial fantasy' of right-leaning groups while leveraging

Girls and women holding and creating space 37

its own anti-egalitarian paranoia. … It may have been that the blithe surfiness of early skateboarding masked its suspicion of outsiders – of anyone, that is, who doesn't skate – as well as its predilection for clique formation against a sometimes (though not always) invisible regulatory bogeyman.[89]

As the political climate evolved, a connection developed between skateboarding and punk, as is discussed by Konstantin Butz in Huck. Butz compares the 1970s economic and social decline experienced in the UK and the USA, each of which bore governments led by Margaret Thatcher and Ronald Reagan respectively, who both adopted political strategies of 'deregulation and privatisation'.[90]

Skateboarding's subcultural years throughout the 1980s and 1990s were typified by skateboarders' anti-social and anti-authoritarian mentality mixed with a residual identification with hetero-masculinity, which was achieved through an amplified objectification of the female form. At the same time, women in skateboarding were organising solidarity groups, raising their visibility, and – through persistence and mettle – garnering respect from core skateboarders. This is not to say that women were unified in skateboarding historically, and it is important to highlight the different feminal subjectivities that were and continue to be contained within skateboarding culture.

In feminism, the idea of having a historically unified movement is untenable, as has been contested particularly within the field of critical race feminism,[91] which is rooted in critical race theory and the discourse of intersectionality popularised by Kimberlé Crenshaw.[92] The idea of a unified feminism often serves to overwrite the multiplicity of voices and practices that have been situated within feminism, and I would not wish to do the same for women actors within skateboarding. As Donna Haraway writes, 'there is nothing about being "female" that binds women. There is not even such a state as "being" female, itself a highly complex category constructed in contested sexual scientific discourse and other social practices'.[93] If 'female' can be understood more accurately as a complex social category, then 'girl' and 'woman' might be decoupled from a discourse of essentialism toward its adoption as a meaningful symbol.

The work of undoing or dismantling gendered systems of power is understood to be in the move from binaries to multiples; from neat, simple categorisation to breadths of nuanced understandings of the social categories we have built. This can be seen within some of the practices within this chapter, and it is exemplified in the increased presence of skateboarders who identify as, or support, non-binary, genderqueer, and trans skateboarders. Many

38 *Girls and women holding and creating space*

of the feminal-oriented groups and organisations included in this chapter are inclusive toward genderqueer skateboarders, but there are also examples such as M. Dabbadie's *Xem Skaters* zine, and brands such as Unity Skateboards and Doyenne who more actively support genderqueer skateboarders through networks, meet-ups, and events.

The current political moment is perhaps best understood through a social justice lens, within which mainstream culture is beginning to turn toward critical self-reflexivity.

Implicit in this discourse is the importance placed on moving forward within culture in a way that explicitly critiques the partiality of a historical White, heterosexual, non-disabled, and class-privileged politics. Pirkko Markula's articulation of poststructuralism as 'a political project that considers society as a site of constant struggle for the dominance of meaning field(s)'[94] offers a summary framework that maps logically to the present and what Kim Toffoletti, Jessica Francombe-Webb, and Holly Thorpe articulate as a 'current/post/anti/resurgent/multiple feminist moment'.[95] In the next chapter I consider how female-identifying skateboarders articulate their own politics through practice, in relation to feminisms as an ongoing political project.

Notes

1 Becky Beal, (2013), *Skateboarding: The Ultimate Guide*, Greenwood, Santa Barbara, 78–80.
2 New World Encyclopedia, (2018), 'Life (Magazine)', *New World Encyclopedia*, July 6. Available at https://www.newworldencyclopedia.org/entry/life_(magazi ne) (Accessed 3 December 2019).
3 SURFSTYLEY4, (2011), 'Patti McGee Skateboard Champion 1965 Tv', *YouTube*. Available at https://www.youtube.com/watch?v=xqrD0Vl5Vo4 (Accessed: 29 September 2017).
4 Sharpclay, (2011), 'Skater Dater (1965) Full 17:38 Version', *YouTube*. Available at https://www.youtube.com/watch?v=lRIt3aDX7-k (Accessed 6 August 2019).
5 Laura Thornhill Caswell, (2019), Transcribed interview with author, conducted by video call, 24 November.
6 Ibid.
7 Ibid.
8 Lance Mountain in Sean Mortimer, (2008), *Stalefish: Skateboard Culture from the Rejects Who Made It*, Chronicle Books LLC, San Francisco, 112.
9 Natalie Porter, (2014), *The History of Women in Skateboarding*, Self-published.
10 Martin Schneider, (2016), '"The Devil's Toy": The Evils of Skateboarding Exposed', *Dangerous Minds*. Available at https://dangerousminds.net/com ments/the_devils_toy_the_evils_of_skateboarding_exposed (Accessed 7 August 2019).
11 Slurms MacKenzie, (2011), 'The Devil's Toy', *YouTube*. Available at https://ww w.youtube.com/watch?v=_cj_rFpWuwU (Accessed 6 August 2019).

Girls and women holding and creating space 39

12 Iain Borden, (2019), *Skateboarding and the City: A Complete History*, Bloomsbury, London/New York, 38.
13 Thornhill Caswell.
14 Ellen Berryman, (2013), 'Ellen Berryman: Skateboarding Legend', *Longboardgirlscrew.com*. Available at https://longboardgirlscrew.com/2013/01/ellen-berryman-skateboarding-legend/ (Accessed 27 November 2019); Kim Cespedes in Louise Balma, (2016), 'Kim Cespedes Interview', *Tracker: Forty Years of Skateboard History*. Available at https://www.larrybalma.com/2016/07/05/kim-cespedes-interview/ (Accessed 27 November 2019).
15 Berryman.
16 Iain Borden, (2001), *Skateboarding, Space and the City: Architecture and the Body*, Bloomsbury, London, 200.
17 Gregg Haythorpe, (1978), *Skateboard Annual*, Brown Watson, London, 59.
18 Ibid.
19 Borden, (2019), 37.
20 *Dogtown and Z-Boys*, (2001), Dir. Stacey Peralta, Sony Pictures, USA; Michael Brooke, (2001), *The Concrete Wave: The History of Skateboarding*, Warwick Publishing, LA; Michael Lorr, (2005), 'Skateboarding and the X-Gamer Phenomenon: A Case of Subcultural Cooptation', *Humanity and Society*, 29(2), 140–147.
21 Emily Chivers Yochim, (2010), *Skate Life: Re-imagining White Masculinity*, University of Michigan Press, Michigan.
22 Ibid., n.p.
23 Berryman.
24 Ibid.
25 Barbara Odanaka in Dani Abulhawa, (2016), '"Crack on Wheels": Barbara Odanaka – Skateboard Moms & Sisters of Shred', *Girl Skate UK*. Available at https://girlskateuk.com/2016/01/04/crack-on-wheels-barbara-odanaka-skateboard-moms-sisters-of-shred/ (Accessed 6 August 2019).
26 Borden, (2019), 35.
27 Tony Hawk, (2007), 'Skateboarding', *Encyclopaedia Brittanica*. Available at https://www.britannica.com/sports/skateboarding (Accessed 29 November 2019).
28 Thornhill Caswell.
29 Laura Thornhill Caswell, (n.d.), 'Pipe Dreams and a Skaters Holy Grail', *Reverie Maps*. Reverie, Santa Clarita, CA, 48–55.
30 Thornhill Caswell, (2019).
31 Just Skate, (2015), 'Bones Brigade An Autobiography, Property of Powell Peralta, Skateboard Documentary', *YouTube*, Jan 28. Available at https://www.youtube.com/watch?v=s5kA57IyqAI (Accessed 30 November 2019).
32 Ibid.
33 Hunter H. Fine, (2018), *Surfing, Street Skateboarding, Performance and Space: On Board Motility*, Lexington Books, Washington, DC, 50.
34 Ibid.
35 Porter, loc. 236.
36 Beal, 93.
37 Cara-Beth Burnside in Matt Higgins, (2011), 'Gender Gap', *ESPN*. Available at http://www.espn.com/action/news/story?page=cara-beth-burnside-and-action-sports-gender-bias (Accessed 5 August 2019).
38 Cara-Beth Burnside in Broadly, (2018), 'Meet the Skate Icon Who Was the First Woman to Grace the Cover of Thrasher Mag', *YouTube*, May 31. Available at

40 Girls and women holding and creating space

https://www.youtube.com/watch?v=UzVT0UdC8bs (Accessed 30 November 2019).

39 Ibid.

40 Michael Brooke in Tetsuhiko Endo, (2012), 'Women in Skateboarding: Being a Lady (Who Shreds)', *Huck*. Available at http://www.huckmagazine.com/pe rspectives/reportage-2/women-in-skateboarding/ (Accessed 6 May 2020).

41 Bonnie Blouin, (1989), 'Skater's Edge', *Thrasher*, Feb. Available at https://ww w.thrashermagazine.com/articles/magazine/february-1989/ (Accessed 6 August 2019).

42 Bonnie Blouin, (1989), 'Skater's Edge', *Thrasher*, May. Available at https:// www.thrashermagazine.com/articles/magazine/may-1989/ (Accessed 6 August 2019).

43 Bonnie Blouin, (1988), 'Skater's Edge', *Thrasher*, May. Available at https:// www.thrashermagazine.com/articles/magazine/may-1988/ (Accessed 6 August 2019).

44 Patty Segovia and Rebecca Heller, (2007), *Skater Girl: A Girl's Guide to Skateboarding*, Ulysses Press, Berkeley, CA, 121.

45 Emily Savage, (2017), 'In the 1980s, This All-Girl Skateboard Gang Took Over the Streets of LA', *BUST*. Available at https://bust.com/living/18944-hell-on-wh eels.html (Accessed 4 August 2019).

46 Sevie Bates in Savage.

47 Gardia Fox in Savage.

48 Rachelle Vinberg in Olive Pometsey, (2018), 'Meet the Skate Kitchen: The Groundbreaking Collective Crashing Onto Screens Next Month', *Elle*. Available at https://www.elle.com/uk/life-and-culture/a22686649/meet-the-skate-kitchen -the-groundbreaking-collective-crashing-onto-screens-next-month/ (Accessed 5 August 2019).

49 *Skate Kitchen*, (2018), Dir. Crystal Moselle.

50 Iain Borden, (2001), 200.

51 Robin Wasserman, (2016), 'What Does It Mean When We Call Women Girls?', *Literary Hub*. Available at http://lithub.com/what-does-it-mean-when-we-call -women-girls/ (Accessed 28 September 2017); Carol Dyhouse, (2013), *Girl Trouble: Panic and Progress in the History of Young Women*, Zed Books, London; Sinikka Aapola, Marnina Garrick, and Anita Harris, (2005), *Young Femininity: Girlhood, Power and Social Change*, Palgrave Macmillan, Basingstoke/New York.

52 Maddie Crum, (2016), 'Hey, Girl, the History of the Word "Girl" Is Actually Crazy', *Huff Post*. Available at http://www.huffingtonpost.com/entry/history -of-the-word-girl_us_57bb6915e4b0b51733a53195 (Accessed 28 September 2017).

53 Aapola, et al. (2005).

54 Ibid., 6.

55 Ibid., 33.

56 Griffin, (2004).

57 Driscoll, (1999), 190.

58 Kingpin Skateboarding, (2014), '15 Subversive Skateboard Graphics from Seb Carayol's "Agents Provocateurs"', *Kingpin Magazine*. Available at https ://kingpinmag.com/features/15-subversive-skateboard-graphics-seb-carayols-a gents-provocateurs-part-1-3.html/13 (Accessed 5 August 2019).

Girls and women holding and creating space 41

59 Chavo, (2012), 'Re: Epicly Steamer'd' reply #63, September 6, *SLAP Magazine Forum.* Available at https://www.slapmagazine.com/index.php?topic=64338 .msg1750170#msg1750170 (Accessed 4 August 2019).

60 Borden, (2001), 201.

61 Borden, (2019), 33–35.

62 VintageSkateboardMagazines.com (n.d.), 'Big Brother (USA) 1992' *Vintage SkateboardMagazines.com.* Available at http://vintageskateboardmagazines.c om/big_brother_%28usa%29.html (Accessed 30 September 2017).

63 Ibid.

64 TWS, (2013), '20 Years of Girl Skateboards: What's in a Name?', *Transworld Skateboarding.* Available at http://skateboarding.transworld.net/videos/20-years -of-girl-skateboards-whats-in-a-name/ (Accessed 10 October 2017).

65 Stephen Cox, (2015), '20 Years of Girl Chocolate Interviews – Megan Baltimore', *Sidewalk.* Available at https://sidewalkmag.com/skateboard-news/ 20-years-of-girl-chocolate-interviews-megan-baltimore.html#lMoO6TIHMic R6Gpq.97 (Accessed 2 August 2019).

66 Dani Abulhawa, (2008), 'Female Skateboarding: Re-writing Gender', *Platform Postgraduate e-Journal of Theatre and Performing Arts*, 3(1), 56–72.

67 Porter, loc. 148.

68 Jilleen Liao, (2018), 'Catching Up with Jaime Reyes, the Forgotten East Coast Pioneer', *Jenkem.* Available at http://www.jenkemmag.com/home/2018/09/05/ catching-jaime-reyes-forgotten-east-coast-pioneer/ (Accessed 5 August 2019).

69 Abulhawa, (2008).

70 *Underexposed: A Women's Skateboarding Documentary,* (2015), Dir. Amelia Brodka.

71 Anthony Pappalardo, (2017), 'Bigotry in Skateboarding: Embrace the Art, Reject the Hate', *Kingpin Skateboarding.* Available at https://kingpinmag.c om/features/bigotry-skateboarding-embrace-art-reject-hate.html (Accessed 10 October 2017).

72 Marlena Medford, (2012), 'Cara-Beth Burnside: Skateboard Pioneer Shaping the Next Generation of Female Pros', *Patch.* Available at https://patch.com/ california/encinitas/cara-beth-burnside-skateboard-pioneer-continues-to-tr895 7ca4861 (Accessed 7 August 2019).

73 Peter Yoon, (2006), 'For Women, It's Nearly Ex Games', *Los Angeles Times,* Aug 3. Available at https://www.latimes.com/archives/la-xpm-2006-aug-03 -sp-xwomen3-story.html (Accessed 7 August 2019); Nate Peterson, (2008), 'Equal Prize Money for Men, Women at Aspen Winter X Games', *The Aspen Times,* Oct 29. Available at https://www.aspentimes.com/news/equal-prize -money-for-men-women-at-aspen-winter-x-games/ (Accessed 7 August 2019).

74 Alana Glass, (2015), 'Street League Skateboarding: An Inside Look', *Forbes,* Oct 12. Available at https://www.forbes.com/sites/alanaglass/2015/10/12/stre et-league-skateboarding-an-inside-look/#1f94cb60677b (Accessed 7 August 2019).

75 Welcome Skateboards, (2015), 'About', *Welcome Skateboards.* Available at https://www.welcomeskateboards.com/about/ (Accessed 21 July 2018).

76 Stuart Smith in Sidewalk, (n.d.), 'Lovenskate Stu', *Sidewalk.* Available at https ://sidewalkmag.com/longform/stu-lovenskate-interview#XEIYK9he22SVpJi1. 97 (Accessed 29 September 2017).

42 *Girls and women holding and creating space*

77 Lisa Whitaker in Broadly, (2018), 'Meet the Filmmaker Who Spent 25 Years Documenting Women in Skate', *YouTube*, July 19. Available at https://www.you tube.com/watch?v=5Zyk2hE6zJk (Accessed 7 August 2019).

78 Marian Wright Edelman, (2015), 'It's Hard To Be What You Can't See', *Children's Defense Fund*, Aug 21. Available at https://www.childrensdefense.org /child-watch-columns/health/2015/its-hard-to-be-what-you-cant-see/ (Accessed 7 August 2019); Kim Woozy in TEDx Talks, (2013), 'If She Can Do It, So Can I |Kim Woozy|TEDxAmericasfinestcity', *YouTube*, Nov 13. Available at https:// www.youtube.com/watch?v=fA2ZHdkw_t4 (Accessed 7 August 2019).

79 Stephanie Battieste in Vice, (2018), 'Meet the Woman Working to Create More Opportunities for Other Women in Skateboarding', *Vice*. Available at https://ww w.youtube.com/watch?v=Az-sD2zsePg (Accessed 7 August 2019).

80 Plotbox, (2006), 'Skate Witches', *YouTube*, Oct 25. Available at https://www .youtube.com/watch?v=Az-sD2zsePg (Accessed 7 August 2019).

81 Kristin Ebeling, (2017), 'Prettaaay, Pretty, Prettttyy Good', *Skate Witches*, 7, May.

82 Baumgardner and Richards, 2004: 60

83 Nav Gill, (2018), 'Meet Lena, the 64-Year-Old Skateboarder Who's Infinitely Cooler Than You', *HypeBae*. Available at https://hypebae.com/2018/2/lena-ver y-old-skateboarders-interview (Accessed 4 August 2019).

84 Very Old Skateboarders and Longboarders, (n.d.), 'About This Group', *Facebook*. Available at https://www.facebook.com/groups/VeryOldSkateboard ers/about/ (Accessed 4 August 2019).

85 Elizabeth in Time Out, (2018), 'London's Very Old Skateboarders | City Secrets | Time Out', *YouTube*. Available at https://www.youtube.com/watch?v=BAxvJ5 -NL1c (Accessed 4 August 2019).

86 Barbara Odanaka in Dani Abulhawa, (2016), '"Crack on Wheels": Barbara Odanaka – Skateboard Moms and Sisters of Shred', *Girl Skate UK*, Jan 4. Available at https://girlskateuk.com/2016/01/04/crack-on-wheels-barbara-o danaka-skateboard-moms-sisters-of-shred/ (Accessed 4 August 2019).

87 Yochim, (2010).

88 *Dogtown and Z-Boys*, (2001).

89 Hanson O'Haver, (2018), 'A Crime and a Pastime: The Paranoid Style of American Skateboarding', *The Baffler*, July. Available at https://thebaffler.com/ outbursts/a-crime-and-a-pastime-ohaver (Accessed 6 August 2019).

90 Konstantin Butz, (2011), 'Skate Punk: The Californian Safety Pin', *Huck*, March 17. Available at https://www.huckmag.com/perspectives/reportage-2/s kate-punk/ (Accessed 7 August 2019).

91 Adrien Katherine Wing, (2003), 'Introduction' in A. K. Wing, (ed.), *Critical Race Feminism: A Reader* (Second Edition), New York University Press, New York/London, 1–22.

92 Kimberlé Williams Crenshaw, (1995), 'Mapping the Margins: Intersectionality, Identity Politics, and Violence Against Women of Color' in K. Crenshaw, N. Gotanda, G. Peller, and K. Thomas, (eds.), *Critical Race Theory: The Key Writings that Formed the Movement*, The New York Press, New York, 357–383.

93 Donna Haraway, (2006), 'A Cyborg Manifesto: Science, Technology and Socialist-Feminism in the Late 20th Century' in J. Weiss, J. Nolan, J. Hunsinger, and P. Trifonas, (eds.), *The International Handbook of Virtual Learning Environments*, Springer, Dordrecht, 117–158, 115.

Girls and women holding and creating space 43

94 Pirkko Markula, (2018), 'Poststructuralist Feminism in Sport and Leisure Studies' in L. Mansfield, J. Caudwell, B. Wheaton, and B. Watson, (eds.), *The Palgrave Handbook of Feminism and Sport, Leisure and Physical Education*, Palgrave Macmillan, London, 393–408, 394.

95 Kim Toffoletti, Jessica Francombe-Webb, and Holly Thorpe, (2018), 'Femininities, Sport and Physical Culture in Postfeminist, Neoliberal Times' in K. Toffoletti, H. Thorpe, and J. Francombe-Webb, (eds.), *New Sporting Femininities: Embodied Politics in Postfeminist Times*, Palgrave Macmillan, London, 1–20, 2.

2 Skateboarding and feminism

At the grassroots level, girl's and women's skateboarding groups do not tend to explicitly articulate a public feminist position, with the exception of Arianna Gil of the Brujas, a New York-based (Bronx) skate crew, who has described the group as 'intersectional feminists'.[1] In personal discussions with representatives from Jerusalem Skater Girls (Israel), Nefarious Crew (UK), and Girl is NOT a 4 Letter Word (USA) in which I asked each participant whether they considered themselves to be feminists, a range of viewpoints were apparent. Paola Ruiloba (Jerusalem Skater Girls) suggested that the term was simply not important; she explained,

> I don't know if I consider myself as a feminist, but what I can say is that I really want to support the girls. It's not a thing about being feminist, it's about how good can you be with yourself that you can help others to do the same.[2]

Rachael Sherlock (Nefarious Crew) equally offers some hesitation towards the term, stating, 'I guess I'm a feminist',[3] and rather than referring to social/spatial barriers in skateboarding or the social politics around idealised femininity, she discusses feminism in the context of economic equality (pay and funding). She explains,

> [t]he girls scene is developing rapidly and the level of young girl skaters is now challenging the level of boys the same age. I think this is a really promising generation emerging that could definitely have a strong case for equal pay in competitions and push more funding for the women's scene.[4]

For Sherlock, a case for economic equality is necessarily tied to the skill level of participants. On the other hand, Cindy Whitehead (founder of Girl is NOT a 4 Letter Word) understands feminism as having a much broader

Skateboarding and feminism 45

function. She answered, 'YES Absolutely – to me it means standing up for your rights and being counted as EQUAL'.[5] This resounding affirmative response situates feminism as a basic human right and umbrella for the range of issues that relate to rights and equality.

This chapter considers the proximity of skateboarders to feminist politics, through analysis of current, centralised personalities and perspectives as they are elaborated in skateboarding populist discourse, videos, and interviews. The methodological approach here pertains to the unpacking of the current moment in skateboarding culture in relation to its context both within skateboarding culture and in the mainstream. This chapter draws upon the experiences and opinions of several world-renowned skateboarders who identify as or are positioned proximally to the gender category of women. My analysis considers these experiences and opinions in relation to academic literature on feminal skateboarders' connections to feminist politics.

Separatism

The cover of *Skateism*'s inaugural issue in January 2018 depicts a head and torso photograph of professional skateboarder Leo Baker; a significant and triumphant first cover for the diversity skateboarding magazine due to Baker's world standing as a professional skateboarder, their support for women and queer communities in skateboarding, and their vocal criticism of the masculinist skateboarding industry.[6] Born in November 1991 in California, Baker began skateboarding as a very young child, but became more serious in their pursuit around the age of 11. Baker has competed in the X Games since 2006 with one gold medal (2014), four silver, and two bronze. They have won the Street League Skateboarding Super Crown two years in a row (2016, 2017). Baker's video parts include *Please Don't Grab My Boob* (NHS, 2018), *My World* (Thrasher, 2017), and *Meow Skateboards* (2014). Baker's *My World* part was received with much acclaim, having been published on the *Thrasher* website with the statement, '[t]his video part shatters every preconceived notion of girls vs boys'[7] and was accompanied by a stream of largely supportive comments from visitors to the site.

In an interview for *Vogue*, writer Louison Cole articulates Baker's multiplicity of identity, stating, 'Baker is many things to many people, and no two descriptions quite match. Ask around, she's a skateboarder, guitarist, designer, or barista… she's queer, straight, male, female, both, and/or neither.'[8] In the same article, Baker explains, 'personally I feel very androgynous. I'm on the more masculine side, which I've always been completely comfortable with'.[9] Prior to their cover with *Skateism* and *Thrasher* video, in 2015, Baker participated in an interview with *Broadly* – a feminist channel

46 *Skateboarding and feminism*

produced by Vice, with the resulting article titled 'This Pro Skateboarder wants the Skate Industry's Views on Women to 180'.[10] The article discusses the lack of financial payment for women skaters from sponsors, which makes it impossible for women skateboarders to support themselves and justify a full-time career. Baker also raises an issue with unequal prize money in competitive skateboarding, highlighting the reality that investment, support, space, and resources are needed to grow women's skateboarding. As a solution they suggest,

> [i]nstead of relying on this male dominated skate industry to give us space, let's create our own fucking space. You know, like Meow Skateboards, Girls Skate Network, Mahfia TV, etc... if we do it ourselves then we have nothing to complain about.[11]

Baker's strategy here proposes a separatist approach, which seeks to reclaim power by disassociating from the masculine domination of the industry. Holly Thorpe[12] articulates separatism in alignment with a 'radical feminist philosophy... that women should not emulate the hierarchal, competitive and aggressive nature of men's sports, but that they should build alternative models.'[13] In Thorpe's view this has an overall limited effect by not making demands on men-dominated and discriminatory spaces to change towards more inclusive, equality-driven practice, and by not urging the people who comfortably occupy those positions to 'make room'. This positive or 'reclaimed separatism' is popular in practice as well as in the industry, as evidenced by the success of feminal-only skateboarding interventions that have arisen in recent years at skateparks, which have drawn the participation of scores of women, girls, and gender non-conforming participants to skatepark spaces that have previously been almost entirely dominated by men.

The strategy of reclaimed separatism can be recognised as both an expression of empowering solidarity, and as avoidance of confrontation and the necessary work that is needed to make change. It can also be contrasted with another form of separatism widely recognised within skateboarding culture, which I refer to as 'periphery separatism', an organisational principle that arguably normalises gender-based stratification and power, but may be useful as part of an overall personal development strategy. During the 2018 Pushing Boarders skateboarding conference, held at the Bartlett School of Architecture (University of London), the final Saturday evening panel was organised by Jilleen Liao – skateboarder, founder of Onto Sneakers, and community activist from New York, whose series of 'Heavy Discussion' events reflect on skateboarding culture often in relation to women's experiences.[14] Liao's panel, titled 'Heavy Discussion Presents: Concrete Waves and the Rise of Female Skaters' featured professional and

Skateboarding and feminism   47

sponsored skateboarders, Elissa Steamer, Louisa Menke, Jamie Reyes, Alexis Sablone, Lucy Adams, and Mario Falbo. Elissa Steamer, Toy Machine pro rider, three-times X Games gold medallist, winner of the World Cup of Skateboarding and Triple Crown, and the first woman skateboarder to feature on the Tony Hawk Pro Skater series, and one of the most revered and recognisable skateboarders of the 1990s and 2000s was a major headline for the conference.

During the Heavy Discussion panel[15] Jilleen posed a question asking, 'how the impact of skateparks and the popularity of skateboarding in the mainstream has impacted the "one solo explorer" dynamic of skate culture'. In response to this, Steamer talks about her experience of growing up skating the streets, of jumping fences and running from the police, and then she diverts from the question to say,

> I was listening to a panel before this and somebody's talking about how they're like scared to go in, or that like, you know, they face adversity walking into a skatepark full of guys, and I was thinking to myself, why don't they just go and skate somewhere else then?[16]

Therein follows a moment of silence, a few giggles can be heard in the crowd, and then Alexis Sablone, visible sitting next to Steamer, starts to laugh, and a delayed echo of laughter follows from the crowd as Sablone palms her face at what Steamer has said.[17]

Steamer followed up the comment explaining that she feels grateful for having had to learn to skate in the imperfect environment of the streets. She explains, 'I learnt how to skate ledges without bumps to them, and stuff like that'.[18] The delivery of this statement in which Steamer endorses a stoic attitude in the process of learning to skate and occupying the sometimes socially difficult space of skateparks, articulates a widely practised separatist strategy, one that suggests the need to 'toughen up' and re-locate in lieu of having the confidence, skill, and perhaps social currency to deal with the rough terrain of the street and the social space of typical skateboarding environments.

Later in the panel, when Jilleen takes questions from the floor that members of the audience have proposed during the break, an anonymised audience member asks Steamer to elaborate on what she meant in saying that '[girls and women] should just go and skate somewhere else'.[19] Steamer explains, '[if] a woman or a girl [was] scared to go into the skate park full of guys... why wouldn't you just go and skate somewhere else where there wasn't a bunch of guys?'[20] The comment was followed by a pause and then someone from the audience questioned this further, asking 'why *should* you'? and Steamer responds, 'so you can get more comfortable on

48 Skateboarding and feminism

your skateboard maybe and then return to the skatepark?'[21] Steamer's perspective – which is representative of wider skateboarding culture – diverts from gender as a factor of the problem, focusing instead on the skill level of the participant as the major issue. This can be seen as a gender-blind perspective, and has been noted in Karen McCormack's research on inclusivity in the lifestyle sport of mountain biking.[22] Steamer's response and the responses of McCormack's interview respondents are of course entirely accurate in identifying skill level as the major factor contributing to a person's confidence and participation in sports activities and communities of practice. To disconnect this from gender-based structural inequality (or from institutionalised racism, homophobia, economic inequality and disability, amongst others) denies the often subtle and normative, but very real barriers that people face in their attempts to participate in public physical activities and develop their skills. The fact that Steamer has attained such a high level of skill and been able to participate fully within skateboarding culture is hugely inspiring and positive, but it doesn't disqualify the (sometimes negative) experiences of women and non-binary participants who do not necessarily have the confidence, ability, or support networks to enable their sense of belonging and sustain their involvement.

Following Steamer's response, Liao interjected to explain further the anonymised perspective by saying, 'I think maybe the clarification is… why isn't the skatepark more inclusive? Why do they have to turn around and go find somewhere else?'[23] To which Steamer explained, 'I've never actually experienced exclusivity at a skate park myself… I've only seen inclusivity'.[24] In response to this Liao raises the issue of 'normalisation' of sexism and passive-aggressive abuse, and then refers to a story Steamer had told at a previous Heavy Discussion event (Performa, NYC), which she asks if Steamer doesn't mind sharing. Steamer responds,

> I didn't say that I have only experienced inclusivity in life, I said I've only experienced inclusivity at skateparks… when I was a child I was like you know 11 or 12 and there was a ramp up the street from my house, a little wooden mini ramp and… I went there to skate with my friends and we had a great time… I went back like a day or two later and written on the ramp… was 'skater Bettys don't swallow' and I didn't even know what it meant… my friends were a little bit older than me and they were like oh don't worry about it, it doesn't mean anything. … I knew that a skater Betty was a girl skater… and I knew that it was directed at me because my friends were… not telling me.[25]

For Steamer, her relationship with skateboarding and skateboarders is one of inclusive friendship; she has experienced sexist abuse at a skate ramp

Skateboarding and feminism 49

in at least one encounter (that was described above), but overall feels supported and accepted. The critical-spatial dynamic of Pushing Boarders was unique in being an open discussion wherein different opinions could be aired and discussed. The dialogue revealed what appears to be two perspectives – one, as is expressed by Steamer, periphery separatism, that functions as a variant on the reclaimed separatism of female-only supportive spaces. Periphery separatism suggests that women and girls should develop skills somewhere else until they feel able to participate within core spaces.

The alternative to these 'separatisms' on the other hand is a complete disavowal of separatism, a demand for inclusivity and the changing of dominant spheres to make them more accommodating to people who are less skilled and confident, or who divert from skateboarding core identities. Periphery separatism and reclaimed separatism can be understood not as oppositional strategies, but as operating across one another. In practice, some women and girls who attend female-only events and sessions see them as both a supportive place to develop skills and confidence, and as a peripheral 'training' space that enables them to enter the skatepark at other times.

At the same time, it is also important to understand the subtext implied by each of these positions. Reclaimed separatism necessarily advocates for female solidarity and support regardless of ability. Periphery separatism adheres to the apprentice-master model of communities of practice,[26] which is embedded in hierarchical gender structures and that places the dominant gender (in this case, hetero-masculinity) as a benchmark. Inclusivity demands the most from core and 'centred' participants to recognise and use their privilege to help and support others entering 'their' spaces. These three different positions can be understood as part of a mixed-method strategy of space-making that is initiated by a distributed network of feminal people who identify broadly around the markers of 'girl' and 'woman'.

Gaze

Baker's sponsorship with Meow began early on in their career. The company was started and is run by Lisa Whittaker and has provided a supportive and creative space for them. Elizabeth Garber-Paul writes, 'Not only did Meow give Baker her own board, but Baker – now a respected graphic designer as well – got to design it. And instead of feeling like the token woman, she was leading the charge as part of a movement'.[27] In 2017, Baker joined the Nike skateboards team, a brand that represents a decidedly corporate involvement in skateboarding, but which has recognised the need for equal financial support and creative involvement. Baker says, 'it's empowering to join the Nike team. It's in the midst of its #Equality campaign. There are

50 *Skateboarding and feminism*

women in top positions in management and marketing and design. My input is valued and put into practice'.[28]

Skateboarding culture has continually argued for the support of skater-owned and grassroots businesses, extolling a resistance to corporate involvement on the basis of maintaining 'core' skateboarding values. In practice this has been largely about ensuring that legitimate skateboarders (and typically this refers to a predominantly White, male positionality) are able to maintain control over skateboarding culture. But this core is increasingly being held to account for its perpetuation of an exclusionary and at times toxic hetero-masculinity. This critical context and female-led movements for equal pay and professional agency in skateboarding have begun to alter the discourse from a concern over legitimate ownership of skateboarding culture, to supporting equality and democratic principles within organisations and businesses. Increasingly, this has paved the way for greater corporate involvement because multinational brands have been quicker and more enthusiastic about meeting these needs, and have more money that enables them to 'diversify' their brands.

Baker's critique of the ways women are marketed in skateboarding was also addressed in interviews with *Broadly* and with *Rolling Stone*. In *Broadly* Baker explained,

> The skate industry is a bunch of dudes making decisions and judgements. If I don't have long hair, wear tight pants and a push-up bra then they decide I look too much like a boy. They don't care about how well I skate or my skill level. It's about how I look. It's about how we all look... 'who's the prettiest? We choose you. ...' That's a whole other level of bullshit. Maybe if I did conform to what they wanted to see they'd give me what I want. I'm not going to do that. ... That's just my situation personally, I don't think that anyone is really conforming; I think it just works in the favour of those of us who are more feminine. If I felt comfortable looking that feminine I would be milking that shit.[29]

Occupying the position of an avowedly queer person, Baker raises the issue of idealised gender in skateboarding. In *Rolling Stone*, Baker talks about their adoption of their own personal style after finishing high school, 'that meant cutting my hair off, and maybe wearing more masculine clothes, cause that's what I feel comfortable in'.[30] They say, 'it wasn't what the male gaze wanted to see, and I think that's part of why I had less opportunity... in comparison to other more feminine girls, they're the ones that got picked, not me'.[31] In the same article Lisa Whittaker recognises that Baker's commitment to their own style was understood amongst women and girl skaters as an important part of their appeal. She says, 'for a little while, she tried

Skateboarding and feminism 51

to fit the mould of what the industry thought was marketable for a girl, and she came to a point where she just wanted to be herself. And a lot of girls appreciate that'.[32]

Baker's inclusion of the term 'male gaze' here makes direct reference to Laura Mulvey's essay on visual pleasure and narrative cinema, which theorises the coding of 'woman' as a sexual object in relation to a centred male ego.[33] Baker recognises that the position of the idealised feminine of the male gaze is unavailable to them; otherwise they would be 'milking that shit'. In this way Baker's reference to the male gaze can be understood as a *contingent criticism* of the gaze and the feminine state of 'to-be-looked-at-ness'.[34] Ewa Glapka – in her article highlighting women's experiences 'in the center of the male gaze'[35] – recognises the complexity and negotiated nature of power in real world contexts and urges academic researchers to recognise the lived experience of people within patriarchal social networks. She proposes that researchers should seek to understand 'how individuals position themselves… outside of academically informed discourses'.[36] Skateboarders' operation within their own patriarchal system and that of wider mainstream culture offers an interesting perspective in this regard.

Baker registers their own feminist politics but at the same time recognises it as a situated political position that would be altered if they were a beneficiary of the system. Though this might be regarded as type of loose feminism, it can also be understood as Baker prioritising support and respect for the positions of other people over the advancement of their own political opinion. It nods to Baker's understanding of a broad feminist field of politics rather than asserting a singular and unified feminist expression, locating her opinion across feminist discourse – and corresponding to a post-structural feminist awareness.

Baker's position here relates to the findings of Dawn Currie, Deirdre Kelly, and Shauna Pomerantz's 2011 study with 20 female skateboarders in Vancouver. Their research found that the girls who were interviewed (aged between 13 and 16) did not explicitly identify with feminism as a broad social/political movement, but they did practice 'authentic individualism',[37] which corresponded to a feminist agenda. The concept of authentic individualism came from the girls' commitment to 'being themselves'. Currie, Kelly, and Pomerantz highlight the ways in which their interview participants positioned themselves as different to their peers by labelling other girls, who pursued a more conventional feminine expression, as 'fake' and not really being themselves. This is the case despite the contradiction that some of their research participants – the 'inbetweeners'– moved across social groups by being flexible with their own identities.[38] Currie, Kelly, and Pomerantz identify that their fieldwork revealed how a practice of authentic

52 *Skateboarding and feminism*

individualism, 'empowered girls to position themselves against a femininity that would subordinate their interests to those of boys'.[39]

Offering another perspective on authentic individualism, Baker shows respect for women skaters who identify in more conventionally feminine ways, recognising that most if not all people are trying to 'be themselves' ('I don't think anyone is really conforming') and that they are not likely to be inauthentically marketing themselves in an appealing way. The research participants in Currie, Kelly, and Pomerantz's study are considerably younger than Baker, and they convey attitudes that stratify themselves from their female peers in what appear to be quite disregarding and unfair ways.[40] Baker, on the other hand, enacts a feminist critique through a simultaneous practice of authentic individualism and collective support. Baker's feminist sensibility promotes a plateau of subjectivities[41] distributing the concept of 'girl skater' across a multitude of subjectivities and situated politics that are separate but related to one another.

Gender regulation

The feminine position articulated by Baker as the idealised object of the male gaze of skateboarding companies aligns with a Western hetero-femininity, which has been popularly associated with professional skateboarder, Leticia Bufoni. Born in Sao Paulo in 1993, Bufoni has won four X-Games gold medals (in 2018 and 2013), two silver, and three bronze, and she was the first woman to place first in Street League (in 2015). Bufoni is a playable avatar on Tony Hawk's 'Pro Skater Five' video game and she has her own TV show in Brazil (*Leticia Let's Go*). Bufoni is sponsored by Nike and Plan B amongst a host of other major brands. She was one of eight skateboarders (and the only female) to feature in The Berrics *Push* documentary (Season 1, 2015). She has also posed in underwear shots for *Men's Health Brazil* (February 2014), and she featured in ESPN's 2015 *Body Issue* – an annual edition of ESPN's *The Magazine*, which features athletes in nude and semi-nude photographs, often in settings that illustrate their respective athletic fields.

Sam Haddad, writing for *Cooler Magazine* – an online channel that documents female board sports and culture – responded to Bufoni's *Men's Health Brazil* feature with an article subtitled 'HELP Skaters are getting semi-naked too', which questions the growth in extreme sportswomen 'using their sexuality to sell themselves'.[42] Questions were also raised following Bufoni's photographs in ESPN's *Body Issue*. Tash writing for *Girl Skate UK* wrote,

> by appearing naked in the body issue she appeals to what many teenage boys are fed as a sexual fantasy, which sexualises females in

Skateboarding and feminism 53

skateboarding and stops it being about skill and ability in the way it is with guys' skateboarding.[43]

Cooler Magazine highlighted the context of the ESPN issue, stating,

> many argue (quite rightly) that getting naked and posing with a skateboard is degrading to women and undermines them. But then others say, because the *Body Issue* depicts a mixture of men and women, it's an appreciation of the human form, regardless of gender.[44]

In contrast, Cindy Whitehead – former professional skateboarder and founder of 'Girl Is NOT A 4 Letter Word' wrote, '[Leticia Bufoni] looks strong and gorgeous and speaks about what it's like to train hard, keep her body strong and skate'.[45] Whilst blogger, Gravity's Child, discusses the issue of 'slut shaming' towards Bufoni, discussing the non-titillating tone of the ESPN *Body Issue*, and acknowledges a Western social context in which 'a naked woman will be regarded as a sexual object… and define her in a way it really doesn't for men'.[46]

These debates identify the interacting realms within which personal responsibility is regulated. These are 'the community', 'the personal', and 'the mainstream'. In terms of 'the community', personal responsibility regulation manifests as concern over what effect Bufoni's career will have on the perception of women skateboarders and their ability within skateboarding. Secondly, 'the personal' is explored through questions over how much power Bufoni assumes in the specific presentation of her images, and thirdly, 'the mainstream', questions what effect the images will have on a general perception of women's bodies. When asked about these kinds of photoshoots by interviewer Mackenzie Eisenhour in *Transworld Skateboarding* magazine, Bufoni explains,

> I started getting offers to be in magazines. … Not in skateboarding but from outside skateboarding. After I did my first one, I just liked it. I liked doing it. It was just fun, you know?… I know a lot of people talk shit because not a lot of skaters do that – but I do it because I like it. … It's different, and I think it's good to be representing skateboarding outside of our world.[47]

The edition of *Transworld* in which this interview features is one that focuses on women skateboarders, with interviews and photographs of Lizzie Armanto, Leo Baker, Nora Vasconcellos, Leticia Bufoni, Samarria Brevard, and several others. The edition highlights the range of different perspectives, personal stories, and presentations of self that are exhibited by

54 *Skateboarding and feminism*

women skateboarders. A summary implied in the issue and that resonates throughout is that Bufoni is doing what she wants, despite 'the haters' or commentators. As Nora Vasconcellos points out when asked in the same edition by Eisenhour 'what do you think about Leticia Bufoni modelling?' Vasconcellos replies, 'I just hope she still skateboards. She can do whatever the fuck she wants, just keep skating'.[48] Vasconcellos highlights the importance of recognising that Bufoni can be both – and more – she can be multiple. Feminal skateboarders are held to account for their presentations of self, the representation of other skateboarders who identify as women, and to some extent, the representation of women within mainstream culture. The perspectives presented here suggest a strong sense of authentic individualism as a current (feminist) ideology within skateboarding.

Bufoni's work outside of skateboarding culture can also be positioned alongside neo-liberal post-feminism as a kind of 'diversifying', and it has certainly been lucrative. Forbes recognised Bufoni as number 25 in their 'most powerful women in international sports 2018', citing that she has 3.5 million fans across Facebook, Instagram, and Twitter, and stating that from January to March 2018 Bufoni drove 22.6 million social media engagements to generate $2.5 million worth of marketing and audience reach for Nike.[49]

Bufoni's back story is also compelling. The narrative around her adoption of skateboarding as a child, her father's initial attempts to stop her from skating, his subsequent support, and Bufoni's move from Sao Paulo to California is repeated in many interviews and articles.[50] In an interview for *Rolling Stone* she explains:

> My Dad is very traditional, and was very strict when I was little. He didn't like that I was into skateboarding. I dressed like a boy and skated with boys as well. A lot of kids would tease me and call me lesbian and tomboy. My Dad became so embarrassed and angry that he broke my skateboard. But the next day I built another board. That's when he realised he couldn't stop me from skating.[51]

The cultural context in which Bufoni grew up and first began skateboarding was not one that supported her involvement in what was perceived as a masculine physical activity. Bufoni describes having to prove her skateboarding ability to her father as a way to bargain for him to allow her to continue to take part, by winning her first ever skateboarding contest in Sao Paulo. This experience helped to change her father's perception of the skateboarding community and Bufoni's place within it.[52]

The regulation of women's and girls' bodies in skateboarding is symbolised in a 2009 VICE feature titled 'Epicly Made Over' in which journalist

Skateboarding and feminism 55

and former editor of *Big Brother* magazine, Chris Nieratko, performs a 'make over' on skateboarder Marisa Dal Santo to look more typically girly. He writes,

> I sent an email with a photo of a smiling Marisa that read, 'this cute 21-year-old girl is a semi-pro skateboarder who has never been kissed or been on a date. ... I want to clean her up with a Vice makeover and get her laid'.[53]

In the article, Nieratko states,

> Girl skateboarders aren't hot. It's just how it is. I wish they were but they're not. It's a dude's activity and so they feel they need to act/dress the part of a dude to get accepted. The premier girl skateboarder is and always will be Elissa Steamer, and for the better part of her career she dressed, drank, and acted like a dude (not that there's anything wrong with that).[54]

Nieratko, a highly renowned and respected representative of core masculinity in skateboarding – not primarily as a skateboarder, but certainly as an influencer – manipulates Dal Santo's gender for comedic effect in an article that ironically parodies the identity politics some female skateboarders experience in their attempts to develop sustainable careers in skateboarding.

In the article, Nieratko states, 'girl skaters suck' and describes them as having a style he refers to as 'puffy butt, which is when they stick their asses way out like their jeans were full of Charmin'.[55] The highlighting of women's bodies as generally bad at skateboarding, and the shaming of physicality in his use of the phrase 'puffy butt' functions as a form of bodily regulation and discouragement that may be a joke (and may be funny), but nevertheless scrutinises women's and girls' bodies, highlighting their inadequacy and drawing boundaries around what can be considered as a normative skateboarding body.

It is important to recognise this in the context of skateboarding culture more widely where there are elements of 'piss-taking' and of bodily regulation regardless of gender. Personal comments about physical style, attitude, and choice of clothing are common in articles about skateboarders and are even more prevalent in online forums or readers' comments.[56] *Big Brother* magazine's historic 'Goofy Boy' feature is a prime example.[57] This culture of scrutiny and (often harsh) criticism has even been represented satirically in New York-based skateboarder and art historian Ted Barrow's 'skate critic' Instagram account (see @Feedback_ts). In this, Barrow videos himself reviewing clips of skatepark footage sent to him by other Instagram

56 *Skateboarding and feminism*

users and posts his feedback along with the footage sent in. Barrow's feedback is an intensely critical review of the skater's choice of tricks, their physical style, and outfit, which functions very clearly as a satire on the culture of aesthetic critique in skateboarding.[58] Whilst a reading of Nieratko's article should take this context into account, his denigration does not serve to inflict those who hold power and esteem in skateboarding, instead aiming at a group (feminal skateboarders) whose involvement in skateboarding and their legitimacy are frequently challenged.

In a similar vein to Baker, Bufoni discusses her inability to secure sponsorship from large companies. In a 2015 interview with *Rolling Stone*, she explained,

> I don't have a board sponsor because most of the big skateboard companies will not sponsor girls. Some of the big brands we met actually told us they don't want any girls on their skate teams. It's hard because I can only get a 'flow' sponsorship, which means I ride in exchange for free boards, while the company makes money using my name. I'm not doing that. I would rather ride for myself.[59]

Read beside one another, Baker's and Bufoni's experiences in trying to carve careers within skateboarding resonate strongly, even if their presentations of self and identity are perceived as opposing one another. Their resonance is as 'wilful subjects', in the sense articulated by Sara Ahmed.[60] Their persistence is an act of disobedience and power, and as Ahmed writes: 'the will is understood here as the capacity to enact a "no", the potential not to be determined from without, by an external force'.[61] Their pushing, carving, and swerving in both an actual and social sense enacts Ahmed's queer history of the will. She writes, 'to swerve is to deviate: it is not to be carried by the force of your own weight. ... The swerve is just enough *not* to travel straightly; *not* to stay on course. Oh the potential of this *not* .[62]

Comedic insults directed at a generalised group of people make for the perfect monologic discourse[63] and regulation of people within skateboarding culture. Michelle L. Bemiller and Rachel Zimmerschneider[64] articulate derogatory humour as a form that 'serves to silence groups that already hold little social power'[65] and they explain that 'jokes serve to tell others who we are and who we think they are in interaction settings'.[66] The subject of the joke is always in a double-bind where any attempt to respond to the insult is to 'not get the joke' or to spoil the fun of everyone else. The only recourse to the derogatory joke therefore has to come from someone who aligns with the privileged identity of the teller and this is where the importance of allies comes in. But, allies have to put themselves out of joint by doing so; they have to be wilful. Allies perform a radical act to mis-align themselves, to divert, to swerve from the core. Writing about Michel Foucault's theories of power, Sara Mills reminds us that

> individuals should not be seen as the recipients of power, but as the 'place' where power is enacted and the place where it is resisted. ... Power needs to be seen as something which has to be constantly performed rather than being achieved.[67]

These performances of power can be interrupted.

Conclusion

Through exploring three themes apparent within the political concerns of women and girls who occupy spaces of skateboarding culture, it is possible to see several ways in which post-structuralist theories and a post-feminist sensibility map to skateboarding practices and expressions of female power. Separatism operates at the spatial and social level of skateboarding communities of practice, whereas idealised femininity and gender regulation are more apparent within skateboarding popular discourse.

It would seem that feminist discourse is apparent to and understood by many women and girls who skateboard as a broad movement that corresponds to them and their participation in skateboarding, but in most cases there is not the impetus to own the feminist label. Instead, there is more of an emphasis on adopting a self-defined social/political position that interacts with the opinion of others. For Elizabeth Prügl this has always been a feature of feminism with 'nostalgias for a pure movement' not reflecting the reality that feminism has always been and continues to be "polyphonus"'.[68]

Read from an academic perspective, these various practices of space-making, personal development, criticality, support, and wilfulness seem to operate as a network of post-feminist and post-structuralist-feminist positions that foreground a respect for inter-subjectivity within this social and political moment. Feminism's development is dominantly recognised in academic and populist sources as persisting through a series of 'waves'. Feminism's most recent move towards 'post-feminist' discourse marks a significant point of departure from this history, as experiences and social practices have altered, but particularly as structures of discrimination and cultural and bodied essentialism are being unpicked from feminist histories. For example, the very concept of feminist waves belies an intrinsic racial discrimination, as Kimberley Springer has discussed,[69] with dominant feminist history tending not to recognise the contributions of women of colour, instead focusing on the activism and achievements of White, Western, and middle-class women.[70]

58 *Skateboarding and feminism*

The practices and theories that have come to be recognised as post-feminist have in many academic and populist sources garnered intense criticism for the connections drawn between post-feminism and neoliberalism.[71] These sources have argued that post-feminism encourages competitive individualism (as opposed to collective social action),[72] forms of entrepreneurial subjecthood[73] that adhere to principles of market-economics, and the elaboration of masked forms of gender regulation.[74] Post-feminism is also understood to support social structures that restore traditional forms of oppressive femininity.[75] For skateboarders, a post-feminist sensibility allows for feminal participants to navigate a culture that is historically sexist, and to claim spaces of power for themselves through entrepreneurship and an awareness of gender regulation, whilst resisting competitive individualism.

Having explored the historical context and social politics of skateboarding culture, it is necessary to consider how the physical activity of skateboarding and the social practices associated with riding a skateboard can be understood as being imbued with gender politics.

Notes

1 Arianna Gil in Patricia Garcia, (2016), 'Meet Brujas: The Feminist Skate Crew from the Bronx We've All Been Waiting For', *Vogue*, July 1. Available at https://www.vogue.com/article/brujas-feminist-skate-crew (Accessed 21 March 2019).
2 Paola Ruiloba, (2018), 'Interview', September 21.
3 Rachael Sherlock, (2018), 'Emailed Questionnaire', September 9.
4 Ibid.
5 Cindy Whitehead, (2018), 'Emailed Questionnaire', October 5.
6 Lacey Baker in Elisabeth Garber-Paul, (2017), 'Lacey Baker: The Rebel Queen of Skateboarding', *Rolling Stone*, May 5. Available at https://www.rollingstone.com/culture/culture-sports/lacey-baker-the-rebel-queen-of-skateboarding-108 560/ (Accessed 24 March 2019).
7 Thrasher, (2017), 'Lacey Baker's "My World" Part'. Available at http://www.thrashermagazine.com/articles/videos/lacey-baker-s-my-world-part/ (Accessed 24 March 2019).
8 Louison Cole, (2017), 'Meet Skateboarding's Stylish, Boundary-Breaking New Star', *Vogue*, April 27. Available at https://www.vogue.com/article/lacey-baker -nike-skate-team-interview (Accessed 24 March 2019).
9 Baker in ibid., n.p.
10 Hannah Bailey, (2015), 'This Pro Skateboarder Wants the Skate Industry Views on Women to 180', *Broadly*. Available at https://broadly.vice.com/en_us/article /jpyzb4/pro-skateboarder-lacey-baker-wants-the-skate-industry-to-start-respec ting-women (Accessed 24 March 2019).
11 Baker in ibid., n.p.
12 Holly Thorpe, (2018), 'Feminist Views of Action Sports' in L. Mansfield, J. Caudwell, B. Wheaton, and B. Watson, (eds.), *The Palgrave Handbook of Feminism and Sport, Leisure and Physical Education*, Palgrave Macmillan, London, 699–719.
13 Ibid., 703.

Skateboarding and feminism 59

14 Heavy Discussion, (n.d.), 'About', *Heavy Discussion.* Available at https://heavydiscussion.com/learn/ (Accessed 24 March 2019).
15 Video documentation of the panel is available from the Pushing Boarders Website: Pushing Boarders, (2018), 'Heavy Discussion Presents: Concrete Waves and the Rise of Female Skaters'. Available at https://www.pushingboarders.com/talks-yt/2018/7/6/heavy-discussion-presents-concrete-waves-and-the-rise-of-female-skaters (Accessed 24 March 2019).
16 Elissa Steamer in Pushing Boarders, (2018), 'Heavy Discussion Presents: Concrete Waves and the Rise of Female Skaters'. Available at https://www.pushingboarders.com/talks-yt/2018/7/6/heavy-discussion-presents-concrete-waves-and-the-rise-of-female-skaters (Accessed 24 March 2019).
17 Pushing Boarders.
18 Steamer in ibid.
19 Anonymous audience member in Pushing Boarders, (2018), 'Heavy Discussion Presents: Concrete Waves and the Rise of Female Skaters'. Available at https://www.pushingboarders.com/talks-yt/2018/7/6/heavy-discussion-presents-concrete-waves-and-the-rise-of-female-skaters (Accessed 24 March 2019).
20 Steamer, ibid.
21 Ibid.
22 Karen McCormack, (2017), 'Inclusion and Identity in the Mountain Biking Community: Can Subcultural Identity and Inclusivity Coexist?', *Sociology of Sport Journal*, 34, 344–353.
23 Jilleen Liao in Pushing Boarders.
24 Steamer in Pushing Boarders.
25 Ibid.
26 Communities of practice theory of Lave and Wenger (1991) and Wenger (1998) as discussed and elaborated by Carrie Paechter, (2003), 'Masculinities and Femininities as Communities of Practice', *Women's Studies International Forum*, 26(1), 69–77.
27 Elisabeth Garber-Paul, n.p.
28 Baker in Louison, n.p.
29 Baker in Bailey, n.p.
30 Baker in Garber-Paul, n.p.
31 Ibid.
32 Lisa Whittaker in Garber-Paul, n.p.
33 Laura Mulvey, (1975), 'Visual Pleasure and Narrative Cinema', *Screen*, 16(3), 6–18.
34 Ibid.
35 Ewa Glapka, (2017), '"If You Look at Me Like a Piece of Meat, Then That's a Problem" – Women in the Center of the Male Gaze, Feminist Poststructuralist Discourse Analysis as a Tool of Critique', *Critical Discourse Studies*, 15(1), 87–103.
36 Ibid, 90.
37 Dawn H. Currie, Deirdre M. Kelly, and Shauna Pomerantz, (2011), 'Skater Girlhood: Resignifying Feminism' in R. Gill and C. Scharff, (eds.), *New Femininities: Postmodernism, Neoliberalism and Subjectivity*, Palgrave Macmillan, Basingstoke, 293–305.
38 Ibid, 298–299.
39 Ibid, 302.
40 For example, Currie, Kelly and Pomerantz discuss their research participants' identification of 'poser skaters' – who wear the clothes and have skateboards,

60   *Skateboarding and feminism*

but who do not use them. Given the financial commitment and social capital necessary to purchase a skateboard, and the awkwardness of carrying a skateboard around for purely fashionable purposes, another possible interpretation of 'poser skaters' is that they are people who perhaps lack the confidence or ability to more fully take part.

41 Gilles Deleuze and Félix Guattari, (2003[1988]), *A Thousand Plateaus: Capitalism and Schizophrenia*, Continuum, London/New York.

42 Sam Haddad, (2014), 'Leticia Bufoni Poses for Men's Health: HELP Skaters Are Getting Semi-Naked Too', *Cooler*, Feb 24. Available at https://coolerlifest yle.com/news/leticia-bufoni-poses-for-mens-health-help-skaters-are-getting-semi-naked-too.html (Accessed 24 March 2019).

43 Tash, (2015), 'Leticia Bufoni in ESPN Body Issue', *Girl Skate UK*, July 9. Available at https://girlskateuk.com/2015/07/09/leticia-bufoni-in-espn-body-is sue/ (Accessed 24 March 2019).

44 Cooler Magazine, (2015), 'Skater Leticia Bufoni Poses Naked for ESPN Body Issue 2015', *Cooler*, July 6. Available at https://coolerlifestyle.com/wellbeing -2/skater-leticia-bufoni-naked-for-espn-body-issue-2015.html#u24gjGwz7xVY ljBj.97 (Accessed 24 March 2019).

45 Cindy Whitehead, (2015), 'Leticia Bufoni Reps Skateboarding in ESPN's Body Issue', *Girl is NOT a 4 Letter Word*, July 6. Available at http://www.girlisnot a4letterword.com/2015/07/leticia-bufoni-reps-skateboarding-in.html (Accessed 24 March 2019).

46 Gravity's Child, (2015), 'Leticia Bufoni and the ESPN Body Issue', *Smash the Skatriarchy*, Blogspot, July 11. Available at http://skatriarchy.blogspot.com/201 5/07/leticia-bufoni-and-espn-body-issue.html (Accessed 24 March 2019).

47 Leticia Bufoni in Mackenzie Eisenhour, (2016), 'Leticia Bufoni', *Transworld Skateboarding*, Issue 381, November, 65.

48 Nora Vasconcellos in Mackenzie Eisenhour, (2016), 'Leticia Bufoni', *Transworld Skateboarding*, Issue 381, November, 77.

49 Forbes, (2018), 'No 25: Leticia Bufoni' The Most Powerful Women in International Sports 2018. Available at https://www.forbes.com/pictures/5aa bea644bbe6f0fa82880d6/no-25-leticia-bufoni/#1f03d4997d1b (Accessed 24 March 2019).

50 Morty Ain, (2015), 'Leticia Bufoni: I'm Going to Skate Forever', *ESPN*, July 6. Available at http://www.espn.co.uk/espn/story/_/page/bodyleticiabufoni/skatebo arder-leticia-bufoni-bares-all-espn-magazine-body-issue (Accessed 24 March 2019); Christina Goyanes, (n.d.), 'Skateboarder Leticia Bufoni is Ready to Roll at X Games', *Shape*. Available at https://www.shape.com/celebrities/interviews/ skateboarder-leticia-bufoni-ready-roll-x-games (Accessed 24 March 2019).

51 Bufoni in Eric Hendrikx, (2015), 'Leticia Bufoni on the Perils of Skating Naked', *Rolling Stone*, Aug 25. Available at https://www.rollingstone.com/culture/cul ture-sports/leticia-bufoni-on-the-perils-of-skating-naked-60444/ (Accessed 24 March 2019).

52 Ibid.

53 Chris Nieratko, (2009), 'Epicly Made Over', *Vice*, Aug 1. Available at https:/ /www.vice.com/en_uk/article/qbz8jw/epicly-made-over-985-v16n8 (Accessed 24 March 2019).

54 Ibid.

55 Ibid.

56 See *SLAP* magazine message board threads, particularly: 'Robotic style' (2008), SLAP messageboards skateboarding useless wooden toy banter. Available at

Skateboarding and feminism 61

https://www.slapmagazine.com/index.php?topic=3468.msg784071#msg78 4071 (Accessed 11 March 2019); 'Skaters whose style got worse' (2017), SLAP messageboards skateboarding useless wooden toy banter. Available at https://www.slapmagazine.com/index.php?topic=8775.msg2667310#msg2667310 (Accessed 11 March 2019).

'Skaters with closed fist style' (2019), SLAP messageboards skateboarding useless wooden toy banter. Available at https://www.slapmagazine.com/index.php?topic=104145.0 (Accessed 11 March 2019).

57 Jono Coote, (2016), 'Big Brother Sean Cliver and Dave Carnie Spill Some Beans', *Sidewalk*. Available at https://sidewalkmag.com/skateboard-news/big-brother-cliver-carnie-interview.html (Accessed 30 September 2017).

58 Andrew Murrell and Steve Torres, (2017), 'Meet the Instagram Skate Critic, Ted Barrow', *Jenkem*, n.p. Available at http://www.jenkemmag.com/home/2017/09/27/meet-instagram-skate-critic-ted-barrow/ (Accessed 11 March 2019).

59 Bufoni in Hendrikx.

60 Sara Ahmed, (2014), *Wilful Subjects*, Duke University Press, Durham/London.

61 Ibid., 10.

62 Ibid.

63 Martin Jay, (1986), 'In the Empire of the Gaze: Foucault and the Denigration of Vision in Twentieth-Century French Thought' in M. Foucault and D. Couzens Hoy, (eds.), *Foucault: A Critical Reader*, Blackwell, Oxford/New York, 175–204.

64 Michelle L. Bemiller and Rachel Zimmer Schneider, (2010), 'It's Not Just a Joke', *Sociological Spectrum*, 30(4), 459–479.

65 Ibid., 476.

66 Ibid., 460.

67 Sara Mills, (2003), *Michel Foucault*, Routledge, London, 35.

68 Prügl, 615.

69 Kimberley Springer, (2002), 'Third Wave Black Feminism', *Signs*, 27(4), 1059–1082.

70 Kum-Kum Bhavnani, (2001), 'Introduction' in K. Bhavnani (ed.), *Feminism and 'Race'*, Oxford University Press, Oxford, 1–13.

71 Elisabeth Prügl, (2015), 'Neoliberalising Feminism', *New Political Economy*, 20(4), 614–631; Thorpe, (2018), 'Feminist Views of Action Sports' in L. Mansfield, J. Caudwell, B. Wheaton, and B. Watson, (eds.), *The Palgrave Handbook of Feminism and Sport, Leisure and Physical Education*, Palgrave Macmillan, London, 699–719; Kim Toffoletti, Jessica Francombe-Webb, and Holly Thorpe, (2018), 'Femininities, Sport and Physical Culture in Postfeminist, Neoliberal Times' in K. Toffoletti, H. Thorpe, and J. Francombe-Webb, (eds.), *New Sporting Femininities: Embodied Politics in Postfeminist Times*, Palgrave Macmillan, London, 1–20.

72 Angela McRobbie, (2015), 'Notes on the Perfect: Competitive Femininity in Neoliberal Times', *Australian Feminist Studies*, 30(83), 3–20; Mansfield, Jayne Caudwell, Belinda Wheaton, and Beccy Watson, (2018), 'Introduction: Feminist Thinking, Politics and Practice' in L. Mansfield, J. Caudwell, B. Wheaton, and B. Watson, (eds.), *The Palgrave Handbook of Sport, Leisure and Physical Education*, Palgrave Macmillan, London, 1–16; Toffoletti, Francombe-Webb, and Thorpe, (2018).

73 Ibid.

74 Mansfield, Caudwell, Wheaton, and Watson, (2018).

75 McRobbie, (2015).

3 Skateboarding physical culture

Skateboarding is an activity that manages to hold together in a kind of dissensual unity a broad range of practices. Kara-Jane Lombard articulates this in the introduction to her edited book *Skateboarding: Subcultures, Scenes, Sites and Shifts*,[1] the title of which recognises the plurality that skateboarding embraces. For example, it is a street recreational practice, which can be performed either on flatland, involving tricks without any additional obstacles or street skating can involve a wide range of architecture including stairs, railings, walls, kerbs, planters, public art, and poles amongst other things. It can also take place on purpose-built 'street courses' that replicate the architecture of well-known skate spots in cities throughout the world within the sanctioned space of a skatepark.

Then there is the street practice of simply using a skateboard as a method of transport, as well as 'hill bombing' (riding at speed down hills), and downhill racing. Skateboarding can also be a transition practice, in the form of gliding, grinding, and performing aerial tricks on quarter pipes, half-pipes, full-pipes, bowls, and vert ramps, and so on. Within each of these practices there are and have always been approaches aimed more towards competition (and within this it is possible to see a contrast between technical skill and approaches that tend towards extreme and daredevil feats), and there are approaches that are more concerned with style and creativity. And of course, there are multiple overlaps within each of these.

Skateboarding physical culture hinges around a skateboarder's development of a trick repertoire, creative expression in their choice of tricks and the ways in which they perform/present them. Central to this is the skateboarder's bodied identity, their choice of presentation of self, and the framing through which they present their practice. The gendering of the skateboarder and of their mode of practice comes into contact with gendered material objects such as the skateboard itself, trucks, bolts and wheels, and the gendered nature of the spaces and places in which skateboarding practices occur and what they are symbolically linked to (for example, the sea),

Skateboarding physical culture 63

whether that is a managed skatepark in a rural neighbourhood or a street spot in the middle of a city. As David Brown articulates,

> it is perhaps possible to say that masculinity and femininity can 'float free' from men and women per se and take on a quality that is simultaneously present in bodies, structures, practices, discourses, and ultimately symbolic universes that provide the material for the ontological fabric of gender relations and gender identity in everyday life.[2]

Gender is perhaps best understood as a dialogic process occurring between people, places, and things in a range of contexts.

Contemporary social media sites have made visible a much broader range of skateboarding cultures than has historically been represented in skateboarding media, demonstrating a broad fabric of gender relations. Joe Moore's 'any skate' project explores the 'creative freedom' of skateboarding and draws from a freestyle repertoire in the creation of highly original lines that use typical skateboarding objects and spaces, such as kerbs, steps, and skatepark ramps, but also more unusual objects such as cycle railings, hay bales, and gas cannisters, amongst other things.[3] In a similarly innovative fashion, Jose Angeles blends skateboarding with parkour in the creation of videos that showcase typical street skateboarding tricks performed as acrobatic stunts. For example, in one video he rolls up to a six-set of stairs and backflips down them whilst maintaining contact with the skateboard, and then rolls away.[4]

There is also a growing trend in skateboarders integrating what can be considered typical or more standard skateboarding practice, but with clothing and associated discursive frameworks that make their practice distinctive. For example, Cher Autumn Strauberry, transwoman skateboarder and punk musician draws inspiration from the fictional teenage character Cher Horowitz from the 1995 film *Clueless*, the aesthetics of artist Olivia Gibb, and grunge icon Kurt Cobain.[5] Cher documents her street skateboarding practice with friends through Instagram videos,[6] and has also featured in *Thrasher* magazine online in a short documentary by Magda Wosinska in which she discusses her experience as a transgender woman and skateboarder.[7]

Relatedly, Stefani Nurding – a skateboarder, brand owner, and model – displays a distinctively 'girly' and glamourous feminine identity through her skateboarding, which she documents on her Instagram account.[8] Nurding's videos show her performance of tricks, often in skatepark settings, and she uses her platform to discuss the relationship between contemporary feminism, body politics, and skateboarding. In early 2019, Nurding became a mother and has documented her experience whilst pregnant. She has also

64 *Skateboarding physical culture*

Figure 3.1 Joe Moore, nosegrab wedge plant escalator ride, taken in Shibuya of Tokyo, Japan while exploring the area with the Yabai clothing team. Image by Rena Kobayashi.

begun to feature her child's integration with her continued skateboarding practice and her professional work as a model.

Despite the range of gender dynamism present between bodies that practice skateboarding, the material cultures in which skateboarding occurs, the spatial settings in which skateboarders' enact their practice, and the apparent potential for a progressive gender habitus, the locating of core skateboarding with masculinity has endured throughout the decades. At the 2018 Street League Skateboarding Pro Open competition in London the media pack listed the judging criteria as: aggressive execution; degree of difficulty; variety; continuity of run; and originality and style. This criterion was also shown on the big screen for spectators, with the difference that 'aggressive execution' was instead termed 'execution/power'. As skateboarding enters the Olympic Games and given the likelihood of Street League functioning as the 'primary path to qualification for street skateboarding at the Tokyo 2020 Olympic Games',[9] there is a need to draw attention to the process by which gender becomes attached to physical cultures, and the symbolic carelessness implicated in socially constructed and perpetuated gender centring.

Liquid physical culture

Whilst it proposes a historical view of the origins of skateboarding, the *Dogtown and Z-Boys* documentary (2001)[10] also represents an origin myth for skateboarding's physical culture oriented around skateboarders' symbolic connection to water. In the film the story begins with Californian land developer Abbot Kinney's early-20th-century Venice-inspired landscape, which led to the construction of canalled roads and created an imagery of streets filled with water. Later in the story, some decades after most of these canals were drained, the Z-Boys began to simulate the waves of the Pacific on the streets of Dogtown. The Z-Boys turned to skateboarding as an alternative activity for times when the surf was flat and they describe how their approach to skateboarding was very much taken from surfing; they would use transitions in the streets as a simulation of waves, crouching very low down on their boards, performing flowing movements and cutbacks, and gliding their hands along the concrete as if they were running their hands through water.[11] Later still, droughts in LA County led to the Z-Boys' occupation of empty backyard pools for skateboarding, which symbolically posits skateboarders as representative of absent water (an interiorising of the theme of water).

One member of the Zephyr team, Peggy Oki, has continued to surf and skateboard since the 1970s. In a TEDx talk discussing her work as a cetacean conservation activist and artist she talks about her experience as a member of the Z-Boys. She explains that during the time that she was skateboarding with Zephyr she was also studying field biology and environmental biology with a particular interest in the social behaviour of dolphins and whales.[12] She articulates a clear passion for the sea, explaining,

> I still love surfing. I've been doing it for over 40 years. … I get a lot from just the thousands of hours I've spent sitting on my board and waiting for waves… of just having the rhythms of the ocean beneath me, and encounters with sea life.[13]

Qualities that can be recognised in the practice of surfing: of patience and duration, flowing movement, and an engagement with the natural rhythms of the ocean and oceanic creatures, are also features connected with these early roots of skateboarding and the practices of the Z-Boys.

Flowing movement can clearly be seen in the practice of Mark Gonzalez (The Gonz), who is regarded as the spearhead of modern street skateboarding, and one of the central people who shaped skateboarding from the 1980s onwards through his invention of tricks and his signature style. In 2011 and for their 30th-anniversary issue, *Transworld Skateboarding* identified The

66 *Skateboarding physical culture*

Gonz as the most influential skateboarder of all time.[14] One of his most well-known and loved video parts, from Blind Skateboards' 1991 feature *Video Days*[15] evidences a clear line of influence back to skateboarding's roots as a surfing practice. He curls through the streets, at times dropping lower on his board and running his hands along the concrete. This general movement style is integrated with a dextrous flow of tricks – often incorporating turns – up kerbs, onto handrails, over walls, etc. such that the overall feel of his style appears quickly paced, fluid, and responsive. His style is not clean, efficient, and linear, but rather more idiosyncratic, unpredictable, and with a sense of freshness and immediacy.

In an article in *Huck* magazine, Andrea Kurland interviews pro skateboarder Lance Mountain about The Gonz and the period in which he came to prominence in skateboarding. Mountain explains that he had constructed a ramp in his own back garden, which local skateboarders would come and use. Gonzalez would turn up to skate it, 'this odd little kid', having travelled from his hometown a few cities away. Mountain describes dropping Gonzalez off at the bus stop after a skate session, watching him ride away from the car, and recognising that there was something special about him. He states,

> it was just the obvious change that was about to happen with street skateboarding. He rode away from the car, up the curb, down the street, the way we would ride a pool. Like, he *rode* it. And people didn't do that on the street back then. He had a mix on what Rodney [Mullen] was doing with freestyle, with the ollie, and also with flow. As skateboarders, everyone looked for some kind of bank or vertical wall or something that emulated surfing. So there's a wave, there's movement, you're on a transition and then there's a lip that you can do tricks on. Mark saw that you could eliminate the transition and get from the flat to the top of something and create the same manoeuvres. That's a huge leap.[16]

This explicit link back to the surf-inspired movement of the 1960s and 1970s places The Gonz within this lineage of practice and this is also quite clear within his movement.

There is no explicit discussion within *Dogtown and Z-Boys* of the difference in style between the Z-Boys approach to skateboarding and more mainstream skateboarding practice of the time, however, this becomes apparent in the story when they attend the Del Mar national skateboarding contest in 1975. At this event the competitive arena included a large plywood ramp for slalom racing and a small, flat wooden platform for freestyle tricks.[17] The Z-Boys are described as having developed a style quite removed from

Skateboarding physical culture 67

these practices appearing 'like a hockey team going to a figure skating contest'.[18] The physical styles presented by the Z-Boys and those exhibited by freestyle participants can both equally be regarded as having features typically associated with the feminine, but the enduring narrative presented primarily throughout the film suggests a desire to set the Z-Boys apart from their contemporaries through gender-association with the typically masculine, tough, and physically aggressive practice of hockey. The concept of the skateboarding team or the collective here functions as a homogenising of physical display and it represents an all-encompassing narrative that sits uncomfortably alongside skateboarders' identification with individuality.

Struggle at the limits

Transcending the body's limits of physical movement is a central aspect of skateboarding physical culture. Professional skateboarder, Tony Hawk explains:

> When I first went to the skatepark and I literally saw people flying out of swimming pools… that spoke to all of my desires in terms of being a daredevil and being active and doing something creative… I'd set out to learn to fly, that was it.[19]

This is echoed in the way he describes the backside ollie as a favourite trick because it 'feels like you're kind of cheating physics'.[20] Skateboarders regularly perform physical activities that go beyond the scope of normative use of public space and bodily comportment. These activities necessarily come with an element of physical risk-taking and potential injury.

Photographs and video footage of skateboarding have, for decades, been the primary means of dissemination of skateboarding practice. In more recent years and with the advent of social media technologies, platforms such as Instagram and YouTube have become increasingly centralised as spaces of transmission of the physical practice from one skateboarder to another, offering an immediacy and broader reach than traditional video distribution through physical copies. In all forms and across participant range (from complete beginners to professionals) skateboarders frequently display the performance of tricks within a visual narrative of physical struggle and hard work, often documenting several failed attempts at a trick as well as their success.

Zero Skateboard's *Cold War* (2013) in a style typical of skateboarding footage from the 1990s and 2000s opens with nearly two minutes of 'struggle', depicting numerous falls, altercations with security persons, and at 53 seconds into the video sponsored skateboarder Tommy Sandoval is pictured

68 *Skateboarding physical culture*

seeming to mentally berate/prepare himself for an upcoming trick.[21] In a different example during March 2019 an Instagram video posted by skateboarder Aurora Dee went viral (with 28,197 views at the time of writing), showing Aurora slip and fall (often in quite comedic fashion) more than ten times whilst attempting to ride up and out of a 'pole jam' with a large puddle in front of it in Brixton, London.[22] Aurora's post received hundreds of positive comments. Representing a distinctive visual cultural phenomenon, it is interesting to consider the corresponding physical culture that has become connected to this practice and the ways in which these different forms of struggle are framed.

Defined as a commitment to succeed in spite of adverse conditions – struggle and risk-taking are key markers of dominant skateboarder authenticity. In 2009, Matthew Atencio, Becky Beal, and Charlene Wilson published research findings on street skateboarders' operation of risk-taking (going beyond the limits of the body and putting the body at risk of harm). They found that both men and women skateboarders actively chose to embody risk-taking behaviour and that their authenticity as skateboarders was closely tied to this. Responses they received from interviewees suggested that

> the embodiment of risk-taking dispositions worked as the primary social mechanism through which gendered skaters became positioned as either legitimate or inauthentic.[23]

Skateboarding is an activity in which participants are likely to experience minor injury at regular points throughout their practice, but it is important to understand injury prevalence to put these findings into context. Alex Dumas and Sophie Laforest published research in 2009 that explored skateboarders' levels of injury.[24] They conducted 388 days of direct observation alongside 23 interviews with male and female skaters at 11 different skateparks in Montreal, Canada, and discovered a very low incidence of physical injury. They write,

> [o]n-site observations revealed that 31 injuries occurred over the course of 35 days. A large majority of these were minor (bruises, scratches, cuts) ($n = 23$), with only 2 fractures and 2 serious sprains so that, of a total of 422 different skaters registered in the 11 parks, less than 1% sustained an injury needing medical attention during the data collection.[25]

Through their analysis of participant interviews, they also discovered that skateboarders learn about their bodily limitations and approach new tricks and movement with caution and calculated risk. There is a process of bodily

Skateboarding physical culture 69

understanding learnt through the process of skateboarding and getting occasional minor injuries that raises greater awareness and understanding of physical ability. They write,

> by being exposed to skateboarding injuries, and by frequently being reminded of their consequences through minor injuries (scrapes and scratches), skaters gained novel insights on prevention. ... [B]y self-evaluating their physical limits and by learning new skills, skaters reduced their risks of injury, developing an ethos of prevention through practice.[26]

These findings conflict to some extent with the appearance of falls in skateboarding. Slams are often accompanied by audible responses (groans and shouts from the injured skater as well as expressions of shared pain/concern from onlookers) that make them appear more serious than minor. Sponsored and professional skateboarders are more likely to be encouraged or to personally choose to go beyond their physical limits, but these falls can also be understood as part of a performance of skateboarding – not entirely fabricated, but not entirely true – that reproduces a masculine trope of stoicism and physical endurance.

An interview with former professional skateboarder Marissa Dal Santo from *Jenkem* lends another perspective. Discussing her sponsorship with Zero, a company founded by professional US skateboarder Jamie Thomas in 1996, Dal Santo talks about being encouraged to re-shoot tricks despite serious injury. She explains,

> Another time I crooked this straight out rail. I landed it a little sketchy and pretty much broke my foot and ankle in the process. My buddy Matt who was filming me said 'If you want him to use that you should probably do it again'. I was stressing out hard. Like, are you fucking kidding me? But I was already so far gone with the trick and my adrenaline was juicing. Luckily I landed it again not long after and they used that one, but I couldn't skate for five months after that.[27]

In this instance Dal Santo was encouraged to mask what was a serious injury for the sake of capturing a smoother performance of her trick. It is relevant to note that part of her decision to leave Zero was motivated by not wanting to feel pressured to do things she didn't want to do.[28]

In terms of recognising skateboarding physical culture in relation to gender, transcending bodily limits can be understood along two complementary planes of masculinity – one involves the performance of falls and explicit representation of pain as a symbol of stoicism, and another involves

70 *Skateboarding physical culture*

the skateboarder masking actual pain to achieve a performance of smooth movement and bodily control. Whilst not implicating every skateboarding company or manager-skateboarder relationship, it would be inappropriate not to register the level of harm inherent in this framework.

Within this context, Aurora Dee's viral video does not completely signify an adherence to the dominant gendered display of physical stoicism and struggle. With its comedic and self-derisory tone Dee's performance satirises the conventional show of machismo by undermining the seriousness and importance of her endeavour. It is a subtle nod to and mockery of convention. This kind of performance is not unusual but is primarily seen within the everyday or amateur skateboarding context captured through user-generated Instagram content, rather than professionally produced skate parts, which are distributed by companies or skateboarding media platforms. For example, in an Instagram post on June 27th by professional skateboarder Jenn Soto, she completes a trick line with the skateboard slipping out from underneath her. From her fall into a lay down position on her front Soto looks up at the filmer and then proceeds to perform 'the worm' dance move before getting up.[29] These moments can be considered as under-cutting the traditionally masculine trait of earnest physical display in skateboarding physical culture.

Technique and bodily-kinaesthetic intelligence

Tony Hawk is one of the most recognisable professional skateboarders in the world and someone who has had a profound impact on the development and popularity of skateboarding. Hawk began skateboarding at the age of nine, after his brother gave him his old skateboard to play with.[30] Having grown up in California, Hawk's formative skateboarding years were in San Diego, at the Oasis Skatepark. Hawk has described himself as a skinny child[31] and explains how he had to adapt a physical practice of skateboarding that enabled him to manipulate the board despite not having the weight of the skaters he was emulating. He explains,

> I was too light to grab airs like everybody else… the only way I could figure out how to do airs was to pop an ollie and, once I was in the air, grab my board. At the time, it looked weird… I was embarrassed about not being able to skate like everyone else – other skaters made fun of me and called me a 'circus skater.' Little did I know that in ten years, they and every other skater would be doing airs using my technique.[32]

Hawk's approach to skateboarding was fiercely determined and he had to work hard to devise his own adjustments to achieve what he wanted physically. He also approached skateboarding with a strategic, focused, perfectionist, and

Skateboarding physical culture 71

competitive drive which was supported and developed in his first major sponsorship with the Bones Brigade (Powell Peralta).[33] His attitude was also a point of ostensible derision within the wider skateboarding community of the time marking, as Indigo Willing, Ben Green, and Adele Pavlidis state, a discordant masculinity between Hawk (and other skaters in the Bones Brigade), in contrast to the tough and macho punk image of skaters such as Tony Alva, Duane Peters, and Christian Hosoi.[34] Hawk went on to win (or place second) in hundreds of contests including gold at the X Games in 1995 and 1997. He started his own skateboard company 'Birdhouse' in 1992 and he became the first skateboarder to land a 900 (two and a half turns in the air) at the 1999 X Games. Tony Hawk's 'Pro Skater' video game was first released in the same year and in 2015 completed its 16th instalment of the series. In 2002, Hawk set up the Tony Hawk Foundation, which funds and supports the creation of skateparks in low-income communities in the USA and overseas, including supporting Skateistan.[35]

In a way that echoes the authentic individualism discussed in Chapter 2, Hawk's approach to skateboarding was to find methods of altering the practice for his own body, and of consistent innovation within a practice that was not fixed or defined. He explains,

> I found skateboarding at a time when I was kind of a runt in school and in a lot of ways, you know, within hindsight I can tell that I was bullied as a kid and even when I was skating… because my style wasn't cool… I was weak so I didn't have the mass and the bulk and the surf background to make my skating look cool… when I found skating I found my own voice, I found my own style, and I found a way to be creative in a way that was an open canvas. Skating was not established. … There wasn't any way that you had to perform or compete, there wasn't compulsory routines and I love that element of it.[36]

In interviews and biographies Hawk discusses his desire to fit in with the social world of skateboarding, to have a connection to the skaters he looked up to, and a desire for them to like him, but in terms of his physical practice, he recognised an inherent need for personal adaptation applied to existing technique, adopting a rigorous process of learning and tweaking. This points to the very different experiences of social and physical culture that can be experienced in skateboarding.

In an interview with Mackenzie Eisenhour for *Transworld Skateboarding*, Hawk discusses his personal learning process in skateboarding in response to Eisenhour's questions about accusations levelled by professional skateboarder Tas Pappas that Hawk had intentionally upstaged him at the 1999 X Games with his successful 900 attempt (a trick Hawk had been trying

72 *Skateboarding physical culture*

for ten years) by having someone take pictures of Pappas and studying the sequence. Hawk explained,

> skating is not as simple as watching somebody do something and then go and do it before them... the thing that we're doing is incredibly difficult. And dangerous. And you have to do it on your own.[37]

The learning of skateboarding tricks primarily through visual stimulus is considered to be widely and typically practised but is not the whole process. It may be the starting point for many people and a route into a trick, but what follows is an internalising of the trick and a processing through the individual's body. Jaana Parviainen, writing about bodily knowledge from a dance perspective, articulates this process as 'bodily reflectivity' in which the individual's body responds to a stimulus for action by selecting an appropriate response, which is based on knowledge gained through practice.[38] The resulting performance may look the same as that produced by another body, but it doesn't mean that both bodies arrived at the trick or indeed that they perform the trick in the same way. She writes,

> two individuals may swim using the same technique and producing the same movements, so that the performance looks the same. However, their methods of acquiring the skill may have been different as may be the bodily schema or the body's topography while swimming.[39]

What is integral to the physical learning process in all movement forms as much as in skateboarding is a level of 'bodily-kinesthetic intelligence'.[40] This theory was set out by Howard Gardner and subsequently critiqued and developed by Donald Blumenfeld-Jones to address the democratisation of this form of intelligence. Bodily-kinaesthetic intelligence is understood in Blumenfeld-Jones' discussion as consisting of five main abilities:

1. The internal knowing of one's motion and sensory perception.
2. The ability to reproduce motion – for example, watching someone else perform and being able to translate that motion for their own body quickly and with ease.
3. The ability to apply complete body attention and intention to a movement.
4. Precision of motion.
5. The ability to perform difficult/extraordinary motion with ease.[41]

A central argument put forward by Blumenfeld-Jones is in the way that bodily-kinaesthetic intelligence is typically conflated with virtuosity or spectacular movement. This has the effect of both distancing people from

Skateboarding physical culture 73

an engagement with their bodily intelligence and reducing the kinds of bodies that are capable of bodily intelligence. He writes,

> We can teach people this way of thinking... with the hope that he or she will develop a deep understanding of him or herself as a bodily-kinesthetically intelligent being. When... culture will, generally, understand bodily-kinesthetic intelligence as an ability to perform spectacularly, it becomes far more difficult to educate for that intelligence, as it becomes a distinction between those who are gifted (and can produce spectacular movement) and all the rest of us.[42]

In skateboarding the prevalence of spectacular men's bodies has created a physical culture in which skateboarding bodily intelligence is understood as an activity essentially connected to masculinity. Although anecdotal, during the earliest years of my own skateboarding practice I have encountered women (and men) skateboarders who believed to a greater or lesser extent that women's and girl's bodies were simply not capable of performing certain manoeuvres on a skateboard. The increase in highly talented feminal skateboarders has instigated considerable changes in attitudes.

A comparison between dance and skateboarding practices is interesting when considering bodily-kinaesthetic intelligence and its relationship to gender. Although the practices of different dance and skateboarding styles vary enormously in the way they look and the places in which they occur, practitioners are likely to share high levels of bodily-kinaesthetic intelligence that cover the five abilities described by Blumenfeld-Jones (particularly at the professional level). Sporting activities (including skateboarding) are commonly understood within a broad domain of masculinity, in which the body is seen as powerful and tough, whereas dance practices and other forms of movement that emphasise creative bodily expression are, despite attracting many men, commonly understood as women-dominated and as feminine forms of physical activity. If we accept that persons of any gender have the potential for developing bodily-kinesthetic intelligence and we can cite practices in which women excel – particularly in activities that take place within organised sporting or dance environments – and that require compatible bodily skills and knowledges, then there is a need to consider how social and spatial realms interact with skateboarding to support masculinity as a centred norm of skateboarding physical culture.

Skateboarding and the social-spatial realm

Spatially, skateboarding can be read as a practice that occurs in one of two main types of place – either public or private. Skateboard spaces are

74 *Skateboarding physical culture*

either 'found' public realm street spots, which are areas suitable for but not designed specifically for skateboarding, or similarly, 'purpose-built' skateparks and ramps that have been specifically designed for skateboarding activity but that are open and free for public use and interaction with the general public. Or skateboarding occurs in private or managed skateparks, which typically carry an entrance fee, often have a membership process, that require (to a greater or lesser extent) the wearing of safety equipment, and in which there are employees of the skatepark who look after the park and its users.

The public space of the city or the streets can be understood as gendered in symbolic as well as practical ways. Theorists and researchers on urban space and social interaction, such as Sara Bastomski and Philip Smith,[43] Helen Jarvis et al.,[44] Liz Bondi,[45] Doreen Massey,[46] and Daphne Spain[47] – to name just a few – articulate various current and historic features of city living and working that privilege the rights and freedom of men over those of women, from involvement in different city-based professions to street harassment inflicted by men upon women. Mythical conceptions of the city are also rooted in a gendered dichotomy. Abraham Akkerman discusses the emergence around 5000 BCE of a myth of the garden (associated with femininity) and a myth of the citadel (associated with masculinity), which have been linked with the development of gendered social dynamics,[48] as has been historically explored by Sherry Ortner.[49]

Free to use public skateparks tend to develop communities of practice that operate at different times of the day and evening. John Carr's observations[50] of one such public skatepark in the USA highlight this as he describes a typical day that begins early in the morning with adult skateboarders (in their 30s and 40s), followed by parents with children at mid-morning who use the ramps as slides. Later in the afternoon people of a wide range of abilities use the park and then by 6:30pm the tone changes as a large group of highly skilled male skaters in their 20s show up and dominate the park. These rhythms observed by Carr over a period of months are recognisable to skateboarders and reminiscent of the kinds of territories people operate as they navigate place. Rather than being entirely free and open, public places are subject to dominant rhythms of use that partition – to some extent – communities of practice from one another.

In his research, John Carr also notes how the gender dynamics of one community differ to another. He discusses the early morning adult skateboarder group, which includes a woman named Jessica. Typically, when skateboarders are sharing a skatepark space or ramp, each skater takes their turn until they have had a fair length of time for their run (usually up to a minute or so of activity). Usually when a skater falls (fails to land a trick and is ejected from their board), it would mark the end of their run. This

Skateboarding physical culture 75

means that skaters who are less skilful have much shorter runs and increased pressure to succeed with each attempt, under the continued gaze of the surrounding skaters who are sharing a session and waiting for their turn. In Carr's discussion of the morning session, Jessica's runs take longer than the other skaters because after falling she is supported to get up and have multiple attempts by the other skaters, despite what Carr articulates as a 'breach of etiquette'. In stark contrast, during the evening session consisting of young male skaters, Carr observes less capable skaters holding back from taking part. The group of dominant skaters verbalise their presence more strongly – Carr describes one skater yelling 'fuck' repeatedly as he fails to land a trick – and by 7.30pm the only people in the park are young men. In managed skateparks the space can be allocated to different groups at specific times with parks running sessions specifically for beginners, for 'over 30s' or for 'girls only'. That said, open sessions in these places mimic the kinds of communities of practice that can be observed in public skateparks, with a broader range of skaters using the park in the day and mid-afternoon and then more proficient or confident (often men skaters in their 20s) dominating parks in the evening.

Skateboarding is not easy to learn. The development of bodily-kinesthetic intelligence through personalised technique requires considerable practice through regular use of places over repeated periods of time. The realms in which skateboarding can take place are generally highly public and autonomous. Even in the case of managed skateparks, for the majority of time skateparks operate without coaches or instructors. This is a positive aspect of skateboarding culture enabling the development of personal motivation and responsibility as well as peer-to-peer learning, but it also creates a spatial-social power dynamic that can be witnessed in the rhythms of skatepark space. These spatial-social dynamics also occur within sessions, with faster, more confident, and more accomplished skaters dominating space within the skatepark (using more areas of the park and for longer periods of time than others).

The development of skateboarding bodily-kinaesthetic intelligence, then, begins in the social-spatial realm and in the ability of a practitioner to navigate these public autonomous zones that always already operate through dominant gendered modes of activity, behaviour, and bodily norms. In this sense, skateboarding practices and spaces can be understood as gendered (and indeed bodied through markers of race, sexuality, class, etc.), but this gendering can be short-circuited through breaches of etiquette and other forms of inclusive space-making either initiated or supported by dominant users.

The development of technique and learning of skateboarding is also related to issues of the social-spatial realm. Skateboarders often offer one

76 *Skateboarding physical culture*

another verbal cues to help with the learning process, which means there is a further internalising of language and visual discourse drawn from a broad community involvement that contributes to the development of trick learning. This concept is recognised by Hawk to operate at the level of developing entirely new tricks in skateboarding. In an interview with Daniel Pearson for *Highsnobiety*, he explains,

> there's... a sense of creativity and community-based goals in skating, even though it's an individual pursuit, a lot of things that you learn are things that you borrow and expand from other people's ideas. I call skating a combined evolution.[51]

Hawk understands skateboarding evolution in terms of building on the successes and techniques of other skaters, and he recognises that the motivation to keep trying previously 'never been done' tricks is – in part at least – spurred by the skater knowing that other people are working on the same trick. Hawk has described this process as 'a bit of a race, but... more like a collective effort'.[52]

The collective-social realm is therefore also a major factor in skateboarders' physical practice, and an aspect of skateboarding that is affected by the bodied position of the practitioner particularly with regards to learnt social gender norms. Aggregates of data from meta-analyses and large-scale studies of gender behaviour, although operating at the level of generalisations, show that people frequently adopt same-gender relationships in cooperative and competitive networks. Additionally, the learnt behaviours of 'same-gender' interactions tend to be 'carried-over' into mixed-gender contexts.[53] This research suggests that members of single-gender social groups consciously or unconsciously are more likely to pass over people of other genders. By the same logic, an individual skateboarder who identifies as a woman may feel a sense of discordance or a lack of social 'know-how' in typically men-dominated skateboarding social contexts.

Conclusion

The physical culture of skateboarding has operated through different gender tropes historically. An enduring masculinity is belied by the presence of different bodies and ways of moving that can be unpicked from the overarching narratives of skateboarding's physical history. One of the most enduring symbols of skateboarding's physical culture is its association with extraordinary bodily comportment, physical injury, and pain. The performance of 'struggle' is central to skateboarder authenticity, which is marked by displays of stoicism and physical endurance. In some cases, this may extend to

Skateboarding physical culture 77

actual physical harm as a result of the pressure to perform. Skateboarding physical culture also has a mechanism for under-cutting and poking fun at the seriousness of stoic display, which has been enabled by the user-defined content and immediacy of short, DIY video publishing on platforms such as Instagram.

The example of Tony Hawk's development as a skateboarder illustrates how much skateboarding innovation is linked to the physicality of the skater, rather than adherence to dominant technique. The primacy of technique has the effect of distancing people from a relationship to their own rhythms, their desires for movement, and their own unique bodily processes for action. Highly intelligent bodily-kinaesthetic performers develop their own ways of working that tend to become recognised within culture as 'how it should be done', rather than 'how it *can* be done', which divests people from their own creative potential.

In a similar way, bodily-kinaesthetic intelligence is understood within mainstream culture as something that is reserved for the most skilled or virtuosic performer. A lack of recognition of a broad spectrum of bodily-kinaesthetic intelligence has the effect of distancing or even depriving people from their own movement knowledge and development. This is not specific to skateboarding, but does operate within skateboarding physical culture, and given the gender connotations typically associated with skateboarding it is easy to see how bodily-kinaesthetic intelligence can become coupled to specific gender presentations of self.

The places in which bodily-kinaesthetic intelligence is learnt – public and private skateboarding spaces – operate through dominant rhythms of users and communities of practice. The social dynamics through which learning processes and feelings of belonging occur are subject to a milieu of normative same-gender interactivity. The short-circuiting of these dominant and imposing cultural networks are possible through forms of inclusive space-making, which need to be initiated or, at least, supported by the bodily subjectivities who hold power at a given moment and within a community of practice.

Notes

1 Kara-Jane Lombard, (ed.), (2015), *Skateboarding: Subcultures, Sites and Shifts*, Routledge, London/New York.
2 David Brown, (2006), 'Pierre Bourdieu's "Masculine Domination" Thesis and the Gendered Body in Sport and Physical Culture', *Sociology of Sport Journal*, 23(2), 162–188.
3 Brett Novak, (2014), 'Joe Moore: A Short Skate Film', *YouTube*, Oct 8. Available at https://www.youtube.com/watch?v=aEzChu_rFiI (Accessed 28 June 2019); Joe Moore, @anyskate, Instagram Profile. Available at https://www.instagram.com/anyskate/?hl=en (Accessed 28 June 2019).

78 *Skateboarding physical culture*

4 devinsupertramp, (2018), 'Skateboard Parkour 2.0 – Streets of Brussels', *YouTube*, Aug 31. Available at https://www.youtube.com/watch?v=gM3ZIfCJQ0Q (Accessed 28 June 2019).

5 Cher Strauberry in *Skateism*, (2018), 'Cher – The Strauberry Peach Interviews', *Skateism*, Aug 15. Available at https://www.skateism.com/cher-strauberry/ (Accessed 28 June 2019).

6 Cher Strauberry, @cher_strauberry, Instagram Profile. Available at https://www.instagram.com/cher_strauberry/?hl=en (Accessed 28 June 2019).

7 Thrasher, (2019), "A Day in the Life of Cher", Dir. Magda Wosinska, Apr 30. Available at https://www.thrashermagazine.com/articles/trash/a-day-in-the-life-of-cher/ (Accessed 28 June 2019).

8 Stefani Nurding, @stefaninurdingxx, Instagram Profile. Available at https://www.instagram.com/stefaninurdingxx/?hl=en (Accessed 28 June 2019).

9 World Skate, (2018), 'World Skate and Street League Skateboarding Reach Historic Accord on World Tour and Championship Creating Road to Tokyo', *World Skate*, Apr 16. Available at http://www.worldskate.org/skateboarding/news-skateboarding/1515-world-skate-and-street-league-skateboarding-reach-historic-accord-on-world-tour-and-championship-creating-road-to-tokyo.html (Accessed 28 June 2019).

10 *Dogtown and Z-Boys*, (2001), Dir. Stacey Peralta, Sony Pictures Classics.

11 Ibid.

12 Peggy Oki in Tedx Talks, (2016), 'Allow Things to Unfold and You Will Find Your Purpose in Life', *YouTube*, Apr 28. Available at https://www.youtube.com/watch?v=ycB29FkoylE (Accessed 28 June 2019).

13 Ibid.

14 Transworld Skateboarding, (2011), 'The 30 Most Influential Skaters of All Time', *Transworld Skateboarding*, Dec 20. Available at https://skateboarding.transworld.net/features/the-30-most-influential-skaters-of-all-time/ (Accessed 28 June 2019).

15 *Video Days*, (1991), Dir. Spike Jonze. Blind Skateboards.

16 Lance Mountain in Andrea Kurland, (2013), 'Snapshots of an Enigma: Keeping Up with Mark Gonzales', *Huck*, Jan 9. Available at https://www.huckmag.com/outdoor/skate/mark-gonzales-2/ (Accessed 28 June 2019).

17 *Dogtown and Z-Boys*.

18 Ibid.

19 Tony Hawk in OxfordUnion, (2019), 'Tony Hawk Full Q&A at the Oxford Union', YouTube, Jan 30. Available at https://www.youtube.com/watch?v=jicIk7YpfqI (Accessed 2 April 2019).

20 Ibid.

21 Echoboom Sports, (2017), 'Zero Skateboards: COLD WAR – Feat. Chris Cole, Jamie Thomas, Tommy Sandoval', *YouTube*. Available at https://www.youtube.com/watch?v=ILN9Tc3GT7c (Accessed 28 June 2019).

22 Aurora Dee, Instagram post @auroradee. Available at https://www.instagram.com/p/BvZ5EpaF0WA/?utm_source=ig_web_copy_link (Accessed 28 June 2019).

23 Matthew Atencio, Becky Beal, and Charlene Wilson, (2009), 'The Distinction of Risk: Urban Skateboarding, Street Habitus, and the Construction of Hierarchical Gender Relations', *Qualitative Research in Sport and Exercise*, 1(1), 3–20.

24 Alex Dumas and Sophie Laforest, (2009), 'Skateparks as a Health Resource: Are They as Dangerous as They Look?', *Leisure Studies*, 28(1), 19–34.

Skateboarding physical culture 79

25 Ibid., 24.
26 Ibid., 27.
27 Marisa Dal Santo in Larry Lanza, (2017), 'What Happened to Marisa Dal Santo?', *Jenkem*, Dec 5. Available at http://www.jenkemmag.com/home/2017/12/05/happened-marisa-dal-santo/ (Accessed 27 June 2019).
28 Ibid.
29 Jen Soto, Instagram post @jennsoto. Available at https://www.instagram.com/p/BzOvC8CB2W3/?utm_source=ig_web_copy_link (Accessed 28 June 2019).
30 Tony Hawk and Sean Mortimer, (2002), *Tony Hawk: Professional Skateboarder*, Harper Collins eBooks, Pymble/Toronto/Auckland/London/New York.
31 Ibid., 44.
32 Ibid.
33 Hawk and Mortimer, (2002), 62–64.
34 Indigo Willing, Ben White, and Adele Pavlidis, (2019), 'The 'Boy Scouts' and 'Bad Boys' of Skateboarding: A Thematic Analysis of *the Bones Brigade*', *Sport in Society: Cultures, Commerce, Media, Politics*, 23(5), 1–15.
35 Tony Hawk Foundation, (n.d.), 'About THF', *Tony Hawk Foundation*. Available at https://tonyhawkfoundation.org/about/ (Accessed 2 April 2019).
36 Tony Hawk in OxfordUnion, (2019), 'Tony Hawk Full Q&A at the Oxford Union', *YouTube*, Jan 30. Available at https://www.youtube.com/watch?v=jicIk7YpfqI (Accessed 2 April 2019).
37 Hawk in Macenzie Eisenhour, (2015), 'Tony Hawk Responds to Allegations Made in *All This Mayhem*', *Transworld Skateboarding*, June 19. Available at https://skateboarding.transworld.net/news/tony-hawk-responds-to-allegations-made-in-all-this-mayhem/ (Accessed 3 April 2019).
38 Jaana Parviainen, (2002), 'Bodily Knowledge: Epistemological Reflections on Dance', *Dance Research Journal*, 34(1), 11–26.
39 Ibid., 19.
40 Howard Gardner, (2011 [1983]), 'Bodily-Kinesthetic Intelligence', *Frames of Mind: The Theory of Multiple Intelligences*, Basic Books, New York, 217–249.
41 Donald Blumenfeld-Jones, (2009), 'Bodily-Kinesthetic Intelligence and Dance Education: Critique, Revision, and Potentials for the Democratic Ideal', *The Journal of Aesthetic Education*, 43(1), 59–76.
42 Ibid., 68–69.
43 Sara Bastomski and Philip Smith, (2017), 'Gender, Fear and Public Places: How Negative Encounters with Strangers Harm Women', *Sex Roles*, 76(1–2), 73–88.
44 Helen Jarvis, Paula Kantor, and Jonathon Clarke, (2009), *Cities and Gender*, Routledge, London/New York.
45 Liz Bondi, (2005), 'Gender and the Reality of Cities: Embodied Identities, Social Relations and Performativities', *Online papers archived by the Institute of Geography, School of Geosciences, University of Edinburgh*. Available at https://www.researchgate.net/publication/239856347_Gender_and_the_Reality_of_Cities_Embodied_Identities_Social_Relations_and_Performativities (Accessed 28 June 2019).
46 Doreen Massey, (1994), *Space, Place and Gender*, Polity Press, Cambridge/Oxford.
47 Daphne Spain, (1992), *Gendered Spaces*, The University of North Carolina Press, Chapel Hill/London.

80 *Skateboarding physical culture*

48 Abraham Akkerman, (2006), 'Femininity and Masculinity in City-Form: Philosophical Urbanism as a History of Consciousness', *Human Studies*, 29, 229–256.
49 Sherry Ortner, (1974), 'Is Female to Male as Nature is to Culture?' in Louise Lamphere and Michelle Zimbalist Rosaldo, (eds.), *Women, Culture and Society*, Stanford University Press, Stanford, CA, 67–87.
50 John Carr, (2017), 'Skateboarding in Dudespace: The Roles of Space and Sport in Constructing Gender Among Adult Skateboarders', *Sociology of Sport Journal*, 34, 25–34.
51 Hawk in Daniel Pearson, (2017), 'Tony Hawk Talks Trump, the State of Skateboarding & His New Board with Penny', *HighsSnobiety*, Sep 29. Available at https://www.highsnobiety.com/2017/09/29/tony-hawk-interview-penny-skateboard/ (Accessed 3 April 2019).
52 Hawk in Eisenhour, n.p.
53 Marco Del Giudice, (2015), 'Gender Differences in Personality and Social Behavior' in J.D. Wright, (ed.), *International Encyclopedia of the Social & Behavioral Sciences* (Second Edition), Elsevier, Philadelphia, St. Louis and New York, 750–756.

4 'Skateboard philanthropy'

A somatic practice perspective

Organisations offering sport-for-development-and-peace (SDP) programmes have existed since at least the 1980s. Their aims vary but are often focused on engaging primarily children and youth communities experiencing social disadvantage, or those that are affected by devastation, war, or protracted conflict in activities designed to build confidence and team dynamics through physical activity. Simon Darnell proposes that SDP projects tend to fall within three categories focused on either social, health, or economic development.[1] In theoretical discourse, sport programmes of this kind have been criticised for operating in a 'deficit mode' that regards participants as victims in need of a typically White and Western-centred version of empowerment. Organisations often fail to see or recognise the ways in which individuals and communities already enact powerful self- and community-building practices. Criticisms have also been levelled at the lack of self-reflexive criticality in the narratives used to justify such programmes.[2] Skateboarding has begun to enter this field through the advent of projects and organisations that promote what Paul O'Connor refers to as 'skateboard philanthropy'[3] and the theoretical frameworks adopted to discuss them.

Several academics have suggested that skateboarding and other lifestyle sports within the SDP sector manage to avoid condescension and cultural imperialism, and do not tend to enforce typical gender tropes inherent within a sports context. Holly Thorpe's research into several action sports organisations[4] found that organisers and volunteers within these programmes evidenced a high level of critical awareness of the work they were doing in specific contexts and a sensitivity to cultural differences. Thorpe expresses the view that action sports offer something markedly different to conventional sports within the SDP sector, particularly non-competitive and self-regulatory forms of practice. Additionally, she argues that these practices do not tend to privilege the male body as they are typically focused on the 'gender-neutral traits of balance, coordination, grace, personal style and the

82 *'Skateboard philanthropy'*

creative use of space'.[5] In a similar vein, Belinda Wheaton, Georgina Roy, and Rebecca Olive, in their research into surfing and community development have found that within the projects they studied, participants are not subjected to paternalistic interactions with organisational staff and volunteers, instead 'surfing is positioned as a sort of "freeing" experience which, rather than restore social order works to instigate an embodied, connected enlightenment'.[6]

The fact that skateboarding offers a different ideological framework to traditional and contemporary forms of sport when working in development or community engagement contexts raises a query about the appropriateness of discussing skateboarding within the context of sport. Although there is much difference of opinion within skateboarding culture, the decision to include skateboarding in the 2020 Olympic Games has led to a flourish of opinion evidencing enough ambivalence from various quarters and commentators within skateboarding culture[7] to contest the alignment of skateboarding with the sporting realm.

For skateboarders, sports represent practices that enforce hierarchical order (through parental and coach involvement), dictate training regimes, and control participant behaviour. From a gender perspective, sporting activities are both framed by and perpetuate socially defined traditional gender hierarchies. Historically, sporting organisations have instigated and defended gender-based exclusion and the social networks connected to many sports emphasise heteronormativity. Relatedly, Martha Saavedra highlights the histories that underpin sport-for-development as rooted in European colonial and imperialist ideals.[8] This is supported in Darnell's work, which also highlights the antecedents of SDP as being concerned with individual character and disciplining of the body.[9]

For these reasons and within the context of an enquiry around skateboarding's relationships to gender politics, this chapter explores skateboarding not as a direct contributor to the SDP field, but rather as a somatic practice. The reason for this theoretical framework is two-fold; firstly and most importantly, it reflects the knowledge that has come through the interviews and observations I have conducted with SkatePal participants and the local community in Asira Al-Shamalyia. The philanthropic dimensions of SkatePal are in this way defined by responses from participants rather than through aims and objectives of the charity. The central findings discussed are that skateboarding can help to initiate self-knowledge, symbolic movement, and creative self-expression, which can be seen to have a wider impact within the community.

Secondly, focusing on somatic practice is a strategy for addressing the lack of attention that has been afforded to dance and somatic theories in academia generally[10] and posits these ideas as a valuable set of discourses

'Skateboard philanthropy'   83

to bring into discussions about skateboarding. This is especially important given women's contributions to the fields of dance, somatic practice, and dance and movement therapy (DMT). For example, Roger Copeland has explored how feminist critique can be seen as embedded within the history of modern and postmodern dance[11] and Christine Caldwell and Lucy Leighton[12] articulate the field of DMT as implicitly functioning as a space of feminist activism, 'not so much in advocating for equity, as by embodying it'.[13]

Skateboarding philanthropy

O'Connor articulates that philanthropy within skateboarding should not be seen as the adoption of an externally defined benevolent practice, but can instead be understood as a natural extension or development of existing features of skateboarding culture. Particular examples are the informal peer-to-peer teaching that occurs between skaters, the sharing of food and drinks between skaters sometimes unknown to one another at skateparks and spots, and the gifting of old decks, wheels, trucks, and (as I have sometimes seen) shoes and clothing to other skaters.[14] O'Connor further proposes that skateboarders are, through philanthropic projects, enacting a prefigurative politics (a politics in process) which is achieved through 'participation, horizontality, and inclusion… as a strategy for moulding a world accessible and sympathetic to the lifestyle of skateboarders'.[15]

Whilst the philanthropic aspects of skateboarding culture described by O'Connor are relatively widespread, there are still many ways that skateboarders promote hierarchical relationships and practice exclusion (as can be seen in the discussions within Chapters 1, 2, and 3). I would suggest then that this prefigurative politics is not only acting on the mainstream world but is also strengthening an emergent movement *within* skateboarding culture. It is indicative to note that activist skateboarder organisation Long Live Southbank and skateboarding charity SkatePal are two of the founders and central organising bodies involved with the international skateboarding conference Pushing Boarders, an event which – amongst other things – fosters discussion around inclusivity and social justice in skateboarding.

O'Connor sees skateboarding philanthropy as a response and reaction to the greater integration of corporations within skateboarding and, it could be argued, corporations are primarily instituted through the increase and expansion of sporting events in skateboarding such as Street League Skateboarding and the Olympic Games. He writes, 'skateboarding philanthropy then becomes a way of managing the image and understanding of skateboarding while skateboarding itself becomes more mainstream and "big business"'.[16] In these ways, skateboarding development projects can

84 'Skateboard philanthropy'

be understood to have – at best – an ambivalent connection to 'sport', and a tangential connection to the SDP sector.

Throughout this chapter I draw upon interviews and experiences from three years of research I have conducted in and around the Rosa skatepark built by SkatePal in 2015 in Asira Al-Shamalyia, a town in the north of the West Bank near to Nablus. SkatePal is a UK-based charitable organisation that builds skateparks and teaches children to skateboard in Palestine. The Rosa skatepark is an open play space that is free to access. SkatePal facilitates skateboarder volunteers (who primarily come from Europe, North America, and Australasia) to visit Palestine and whose role is to encourage and help local children and young people to learn to skateboard in informal sessions that occur most days during the week throughout the summer months. I helped to build the skatepark in 2015 and have returned each year to examine how the skatepark is used and to speak with local people and volunteers about how the skatepark is functioning within the locale.

The findings of Thorpe; Wheaton, Roy, and Olive; O'Connor; and Sophie Friedel, together represent a knowledge of skateboarding philanthropic projects and organisations in which skateboarder-initiators adopt a critical awareness and recognise their positionality in relation to the geopolitical contexts in which they work. These scholars highlight the counter-sporting narratives inherent in skateboarding philanthropy projects, which

Figure 4.1 Asira skatepark, view from top of flatbank, 2015. Image by Emil Agerskov.

'Skateboard philanthropy' 85

Figure 4.2 Local young people learning to skateboard in Asira Al-Shamalyia's Rosa Skatepark, 2015. Image by Emil Agerskov.

are defined around the avoidance of body discipline, the valorising of expressiveness, and inclusivity of practice. In this context it seems relevant to look to the praxis framework of modern dance and somatic practices to reconsider skateboarding and skateboarding philanthropy projects.

Rosa Skatepark, Asira Al-Shamalyia

The Rosa skatepark draws participation from a wide age group including a large proportion of young children (below the age of 16) who come with their parents, siblings, and sometimes aunts, uncles, and cousins. There are some older adolescent participants, and several adolescents and adults that come to the skatepark to socialise and watch the skateboarding rather than to participate themselves. Interviews were conducted either in Arabic (through an interpreter and then translated) or in English. Respondents varied in age between 13 and approx. 55 (adults were not asked to give their age). The respondents included some parents of participating children and other people who have either visited or regularly visit the Rosa skatepark. Interviews were conducted during September 2017 (one respondent) and September 2018 (13 respondents) and the semi-structured questions focused on people's thoughts and feelings about skateboarding, their experiences within

86 'Skateboard philanthropy'

the skatepark, and the wider local perception of skateboarding in Asira Al-Shamalyia.

The first thing to mention about these interviews is that all but two of the respondents automatically referred to skateboarding as a sport. Both of the two respondents who did not refer to skateboarding as a sport were girls. One of these was 'R', a 16-year-old skateboarder. When in response I asked her, 'is skateboarding more like a sport or a dance to you?' she replied, 'it's a mixture of both'.[17] Another participant, 'AR', a 19-year-old male skateboarder explained that he was also in a Dabke band. Dabke is a form of traditional Palestinian dance often practised by men (and women), which is seen as a celebration of Palestinian nationalism and has been used as a symbol of resistance during the British mandate and throughout the Israeli occupation of Palestine.[18] AR saw no translatable skills crossing over between skateboarding and his Dabke practice. He was clear that skateboarding was a sport and an entirely separate activity to Dabke dancing.[19] People's use of the 'sport' label here is perhaps more indicative of the term as a catchall for physical activities in general. Indeed, for ease of translation I would often use the term 'sport' myself when conversing with local people instead of the more open but inconvenient phrase 'physical activity', but it is relevant that already within this fledgeling scene that skateboarding shows some signs of ambiguity around its categorisation. I would also suggest that the labelling of skateboarding as a sport may play a part in encouraging the participation of young men who may not wish to identify their activity with 'dance'.

The headteacher of one of the girl's schools in Asira Al-Shamalyia, which accommodates students between the ages of 10 and 15 years, offered a sense of the educational context of sport and dance activity in the locality and in Palestine more generally. The Palestinian Ministry of Education designates 'sports training' as mandatory for all children, but the focus given to physical education varies from one school to another.[20] Dance and performing arts are not part of the school curriculum, but they are practised as an extra-curricular activity. The headteacher explained that sports are seen as an activity that supports other subjects. She explained, 'sports help raise the student's mental activity which leads to better performance in the other subjects they study'.[21] Additionally, the municipality of Asira Al-Shamalyia reacted positively to the news that skateboarding was entering the Olympics in 2020. Community leaders have been keen to encourage young people in the locality to take up skateboarding and develop their practice, with a view towards a potential future national Olympic entry.

This is not to say that skateboarding's creative and somatic qualities are given short shrift in Palestine. During 2015 when I was involved with building the skatepark in Asira Al-Shamalyia, I attended the local girls' school with Charlie Davis, the director of SkatePal, and the only other

'Skateboard philanthropy' 87

woman volunteer that year to encourage interest from the girls at the school in trying skateboarding. Before the park was built, we proposed to set up some skateboarding classes for groups of girls on the flat concrete school-yard at the school. When we visited to make this proposal, Mohammed Sawalha, the director of the Palestinian House of Friendship, asked each of us to speak about the benefits of skateboarding, which he interpreted to the assembled group. I focused on describing the creative and dance-like opportunities of skateboarding. Afterwards, Mohammed said he had liked this idea of skateboarding as a creative practice because it could contribute to improved innovative capability, and we also discussed how concentration and focus in creative movement can have a spiritual and meditative quality. Given the fact that sporting activity is socially understood as a support to intellectual skills, there is little surprise that the term 'sport' holds the greatest social value.

Somatic qualities of skateboarding

As a field of 'creative science', somatic practice has a more than 200-year-old history,[22] existing in formalised methods within more than 37 different programmes that have been developed by a range of practitioners, many of whom were looking for solutions to help with chronic physical and emotional problems, and several – particularly from the early to mid 20th century – who were also practitioners of modern dance.[23] In her article on somatic knowledge in dance education, Jill Green highlights the differences between generalised dance training and somatics explaining that dance training focuses on movement goals, desired postural alignment, and stylisation, whereas somatics is concerned with sensory processing, therapeutic reprogramming of body systems, and person-specific ways of working.[24]

Somatic practices such as Authentic Movement, Feldenkrais Method, and Skinner Releasing Technique (amongst many others) developed from 'experiential investigations into the body's... natural healing potential'[25] and have become formal therapeutic methods used by qualified therapist practitioners. Whilst somatic practice and dance are not one and the same thing, Martha Eddy acknowledges a link between them marked by the ways that modern dance and movement practitioners such as Rudolf Laban, Isadora Duncan, Martha Graham, and others brought bodily sensation and personal expression to the fore of their dance methods.[26] As Green states, '[t]here are ways that a somatic perspective can be effectively brought into dance class'.[27] I would suggest that somatic perspectives are also relevant to the movement practices of skateboarders and can be evidenced in several ways within skateboarding philanthropy projects.

88 *'Skateboard philanthropy'*

Self-knowledge

Firstly, in somatic teaching the practitioner's body is immersed in a given somatic practice and the individual 'discover[s] for themselves what is important, "social and cultural insights included"'.[28] Within a typical skateboarding practice, which is marked by the absence of a formal teacher, of standardised technique (as has been discussed in Chapter 3), and in the general lack of a specified goal, skateboarders actively explore and take ownership of their own bodies. This is not just in terms of the way skateboarders learn tricks, but also in their choice of tricks (or indeed their invention of new ones) and in the ways that skateboarders navigate public or skatepark space by following their own 'lines'. The same learning process is adopted in the work of SkatePal, where there is no formalised process for teaching children to skateboard. Volunteers may come with their own approaches but as an organisation SkatePal does not impose or endorse a particular technique, recognising that each skateboarder participant comes to the practice with their own interests and desires for movement. I would not make the case that this openness or somatic approach is practised by all skateboarding philanthropy projects at all times, but even when projects do operate through some formalised skateboarding tuition, this is usually employed as an initial measure to encourage participants to become more familiar with the skateboard and to learn basic standing and moving techniques, rather than to discipline the body or to specify technique.

Writing about her experiences volunteering for international skateboarding development organisation, Skateistan, Sophie Friedel suggests that the embodied experience of skateboarding raises an awareness in the practitioner that can be used to develop 'self-knowledge'.[29] She writes,

> when consciously paying attention to such somatic and psychological experiences one can gain a greater understanding of one's drives, desires, blockages, and weaknesses. What drives me? What scares me? Where does my contact boundary reach its limits and where can I dare to go further? Can I trust easily or have [I] difficulties to step into the unknown? How can I handle my anger and frustration?[30]

In the Rosa skatepark participants are given the freedom to develop their interests and many choose to test the boundaries of their physical limits, selecting more difficult obstacles and judging their capacity for success. They actively ask for help – seeking out volunteers, parents, and friends to assist with dropping in or rolling in – and they offer help to others, empathising with other users of the park and the difficulties of overcoming fear. Participants experience the rush of joy at successfully dropping

'Skateboard philanthropy' 89

in and rolling out of a transition, and they experience the frustration of not being able to commit to a trick. Participants also witness other people using the park – they see the differing desires, blockages, successes, and weaknesses displayed by others. They see that everyone has different difficulties, and different ease. Their use of the skatepark is entirely self-defined and self-reflexive.

Since returning from her work with Skateistan, Friedel has begun a therapeutic programme called 'Drop In Ride Out'[31] based in Freiberg, Germany, that combines skateboarding with gestalt therapy, a psychotherapeutic technique that encourages self-awareness and self-responsibility through a dialogic relationship between therapist and patient practised in the immediacy of the present moment. The therapist does not provide interpretations but facilitates the patient to explore what they are feeling and thinking in the present moment through questioning, noticing, and encouragement. Gestalt therapy typically involves encouraging patients to engage in body and moving techniques that enable the patient to physicalise their feelings or needs.[32] In this case, the skatepark setting and skateboarding practice are the settings for therapeutic work.

This kind of formalised therapeutic use of skateboarding is not practised by SkatePal or widely practised in other contexts, but there are other related

Figure 4.3 View of the south side of Asira Al-Shamalyia's Rosa Skatepark, 2015. Image by Emil Agerskov.

90 'Skateboard philanthropy'

examples: The A.skate Foundation (operating within the USA, Ireland, and Australia) run skateboarding sessions that are 'friendly' to children on the autism spectrum and who they believe can benefit from skateboarding's typical 'no coach, no team, rip solo' features. On their website, A.skate state that the skateboarding setting can function as a form of occupational therapy for children with autism.[33]

In Canada, skateboarder Joel Pippus, working for Hull Services and the Child Trauma Academy, initiated a study into skateboarding's contribution to the work of the Child Trauma Academy by linking skateboarding activity to Bruce Perry's Neurosequential Model of Therapeutics (NMT). In a video produced by Hull Services, the director of Hull's trauma-informed services Emily Wang, articulates how skateboarding offers a unique social space and activity that meets Perry's NMT. In particular, she explains how skateboarding offers practitioners:

1. A soothing sensory stimulus.
2. Patterned and repetitive movements that regulate stress response.
3. A socialisation setting that operates through verbal and non-verbal means as well as peer-to-peer learning.
4. Through the learning of tricks (and combinations of tricks), skateboarding engages participants in abstract reasoning and complex executive functioning.[34]

In the example of A.skate and in the work of Hull Services, skateboarding functions as a generalised activity broadly suited to social and cognitive development. Literature on the efficacy of skateboarding corresponds to these practices and findings. Graham L. Bradley in his study of skateparks as spaces of adolescent development highlights several healthy development processes that derive from 'unstructured leisure activities' such as skateboarding. In particular, he identified participants' recognition, utilisation, and development of competencies; and exploration, achievement, and expression of identity.[35] What is different about Friedel's therapeutic approach is the potential for skateboarding to be understood as a knowledge-producing activity (through the development of self-awareness), which is derived from and facilitated by movement of the body.

One of the questions I asked participants in the Rosa skatepark was about the skills they were learning through skateboarding practice. Responses were roughly organised around three themes. The first two of these themes are (1) physical/motor skills and (2) emotional skills. For example, a 15-year-old female skateboarder, 'S', focused on the physical skills she had developed through skateboarding, citing her development of 'balance', learning to 'skate on the slides' (skateboard ramps), and increased 'fitness'.[36]

'Skateboard philanthropy' 91

A Mother, 'A', of three regular skateboarders at the park (a girl and two boys) explained:

> the first skill is the intellectual skill because the skater has to keep his balance and control his body in a way that keeps that balance... [secondly] he tries for the first time and the second and the third time until he achieves what he wanted to do. To him nothing becomes difficult. And not just in playing this sport, in the future whenever he faces a difficulty he will overcome it. This sport helped the skater develop intellectual skills and gave them determination.[37]

A's summary of the skills she recognises in her children map across to those described by S above. Participants learn to reframe difficulty as a process of developing requisite skills and not a reason to simply give up. A's recognition of balance as an intellectual skill and determination as something other is also interesting to this discussion, suggesting that there is a body–mind relationship embedded in participants' understanding of skateboarding practice.

Symbolic movement

Skateboarding of all kinds stems from fundamental movements, which form the root of general board riding, of tricks, and of transition skateboarding. 'Pushing', in which the skateboarder propels themselves forwards on the board is perhaps the most basic movement of all which involves having one foot (usually) at the front of the board, above the front truck. The skateboarder's back foot pushes against the ground to propel the skateboard and body forwards and then the skateboarder's back foot is placed on the board, either on the tail or towards the back truck area so as to maintain a balanced riding stance across the board. Skateboarders Peter Whitley and Alec Beck discuss the push as a form of symbolic movement in an episode of the *Tony Hawk Foundation Podcast* on 'Skateboarding as Emotional Therapy'. They describe the act of 'pushing' – with its forwards momentum produced between body, board, and ground as a literal and figurative embodiment of momentum and agency.[38] To push is to exert effort, to compel or urge, and to keep going.

In terms of tricks, the ollie is typically considered to be a gateway into advanced tricks, as it requires the skateboarder to lift the skateboard off the ground maintaining close proximity to the feet whilst the board is levelled out, and then returning the board and skateboarder to the ground. It is the most basic of jump moves and allows a greater range of movement through urban landscapes – up curbs, down stair sets, and over drains and

92 'Skateboard philanthropy'

Figure 4.4 Push, 2019. Illustrated by Jon Horner.

rough concrete. It also enables skateboarders to initiate grinds and slides on objects at height, such as blocks, planters, benches, and handrails. The moment of kicking the tail down against the ground, which achieves the lift of the board has been discussed by Åsa Bäckstöm[39] as the physical demonstration of decisiveness and explosiveness.[40] In the act of performing an ollie the skateboarder commits their body to an energetic leap that requires a high level of self-trust (and the alignment of physical skill with a decisive mindset) to successfully perform. This symbolic movement is also performative – the more it is performed, the more this reinforces the skateboarder's self-trust in their body–mind alignment to allow for the performance of enhanced difficulty and higher risk tricks.

Similarly to the ollie, the entry point to transition skateboarding (on ramps and banks) is to 'drop in', which requires an even greater level of self-trust and a different kind of decisiveness. Dropping in involves the skateboarder placing the tail of their skateboard on the flat top of the ramp with their back wheels and front wheels extending out over the ramp transition. At this point the skateboarder's weight is on the back foot and on the

Figure 4.5 Ollie, 2019. Illustrated by Jon Horner.

tail, keeping the skateboarder balanced at the top of the ramp. With the skateboarder's back foot positioned on the tail, their front foot is placed over the bolts of the front truck (which is hovering over the ramp). When ready, the skateboarder transfers their weight to the front of their body and onto their front foot, which sends the nose of the skateboard down towards the ramp transition. Once the skateboard wheels connect with the ramp surface, the skateboarder is able to ride down and out of the ramp. The moment of 'dropping' requires total commitment to the action – it is a symbolic action of giving up control to the weight and accumulated skill of the skateboarder's body. The speed with which dropping in occurs does not allow for much cognitive decision-making or processing of what is happening. The body must respond through somatic-kinaesthetic know how.

These actions are performed and expanded upon repeatedly within a skateboarding practice and across an individual's skateboarding career such that part of understanding skateboarding is to recognise the somatic-symbolic dimension that skateboarding bodies operate within. Momentum, effort, and agency reinforce the need for accumulated practice and determination. Decisiveness and explosiveness require and develop a sense of the skateboarder's command of the self whilst commitment to the body and release of control values the somatic heritage developed by skateboarders through the thousands of hours devoted to even the most rudimentary of tricks.[41]

Skateboarding grinds and slides, combinations of tricks, and turns, offer further symbols to add to this discussion. I have chosen to introduce these concepts here in the outline of the most basic of tricks and movements as a route into the findings from my experiences in the West Bank. In a previous article, I have explored skateboarding's connections to 'smoothness' and a smoothing of space,[42] which can be read alongside these ideas. There are certainly more possibilities for examining skateboarding's symbolic-somatic dimension in more detail.

Another skateboarder from the Rosa skatepark, 'J', a 20-year-old male, identified balance as an important skill he had learnt through his

Figure 4.6 Drop In, 2019. Illustrated by Jon Horner.

94 'Skateboard philanthropy'

Figure 4.7 SkatePal volunteer assisting a hippy jump, 2017. Image by Emil Agerskov.

skateboarding practice, but also pointed to emotional benefits referencing 'determination' and 'courage'. When asked about what the atmosphere was like at the skatepark, he mentioned the 'fun' and 'enthusiasm' of people at the skatepark, adding that skateboarding as an activity, encourages 'the skaters' sense of adventure'.[43] I would suggest that this identification of 'adventure' can be understood to relate to the 'release of control' symbolic-somatic aspect of skateboarding discussed in this section.

Creative self-expression

Skateboarding is widely recognised as a creative act in which practitioners hone a unique physical style whilst also adhering to some collectively defined ideal qualities of movement. In his analysis of the visual culture of skateboarding videos, David Buckingham explains,

> 'Style' in skateboarding is not simply a matter of technical ability: it is not just about the moves you make, but also about how you move. Discussions among skateboarders frequently struggle to encapsulate these elusive but vital qualities: skateboarding is not only about elegance, fluidity and effortless ease but also about aggression, about

'*Skateboard philanthropy*' 95

defying gravity – and perhaps above all, about what I have called *embodied attitude*.[44]

The expressive qualities of elegance, fluidity, effortlessness, and aggression articulated by Buckingham represent collectively defined physical qualities that are conditioned by the idiosyncrasies of 'embodied attitude'. The widely recognised 'I'd rather watch Gino push' meme illustrates this. Quoted in numerous articles and likely originating from the *SLAP Magazine* message boards,[45] the phrase celebrates professional skateboarder Gino Ianucci's most basic physical effort on a skateboard and suggests his style is more enjoyable to watch than advanced tricks delivered with a lack of stylishness.

Former professional skateboarder Jeff Grosso produced a short video on skateboarding style as part of his series 'Love Letters to Skateboarding'.[46] In this he interviews several professional and former professional skateboarders – particularly those from the earliest waves of skateboarding – to discuss style. The responses highlight the way style is understood as a signature that can be recognisable to other skateboarders. During the video, professional skateboarder John Cardiel describes style as 'a person's energy... expelled on their board'.[47] In a similar vein, professional skateboarder Jason Dill describes how individual style can be so imprinted in physical practice that it becomes possible to recognise, even at distance. He explains, 'if I see someone pushing down the street and they're three or four blocks away, I know who it is'.[48]

There is also a high level of value attached to stylish authenticity. In the same video, Greg Hunt remarks, 'the worst kind of style is fake style'[49] and Cardiel states, 'you can tell what's real and what's added on'.[50] Within skateboarding practice then, individualised bodily expression, fluency of style and, most importantly, authenticity of style expressed through the body carry significant currency. Dwayne Peters explains that this authentic and personalised expression comes from a process of adopting favourite qualities from other skateboarders. He states, 'every skater that you like, take the best parts of that and throw it in and create your own goulash'.[51] Individual style might then be understood to come from the collective field of skateboarding practice – an individualised expression born out of the somatic field.

Relatedly, in somatic practice and in contact improvisation in dance, participants are often invited to be responsive to physical or verbal stimuli, either from a therapist, witness, or another practitioner.[52] The collective spatial practice of skateboarding in skateparks and spots can be understood to correspond within this conceptual framework. Within the typical flow of a session skateboarding involves a process of receptiveness both to the place in which the skateboarder is practising and to other skaters in close

96 'Skateboard philanthropy'

proximity. Skateboarders take cues from their connection to the space to decide how to move and how to create lines, and through peripheral viewpoints of other skateboarders, movements performed by other people and performed elsewhere in the park or spot can spark lines and tricks in others. The somatic practice of 'listening to the body'[53] can be understood to be extended here to skateboarders' absorption of self in space, and to a 'listening in' to the collective body of users of space within a skateboarding session. Creative self-expression then, within skateboarding, is highly implicated in community involvement. Skateboarding is a socially engaged form of practice that encourages self-expression.

In terms of making a connection to skateboarding philanthropy, there is a need to consider the usefulness of self-expression. Many researchers recommend the importance of creative self-expression, but as Marie Forgeard and James Kaufman found in their review of 200 articles spanning four distinctive disciplines, approx. one third did not explicitly address why imagination, creativity, and innovation are important,[54] demonstrating the tendency in academic studies to assume the importance of creativity. Theorists and practitioners in the discipline of performance studies have predominantly grappled with this question over the importance and purpose of creativity. The seminal work of Richard Schechner, particularly his theory of the seven functions of performance (as a term that covers the broadest possible

Figure 4.8 View of northeast corner of Asira Al-Shamalyia's Rosa Skatepark, 2015. Image by Emil Agerskov.

range of human physical activity), derives from decades of anthropological study into human creative expression in a range of contexts including in the arts, everyday life, therapeutic spaces, education, business, and religious settings. His seven functions are to entertain, to make something beautiful, to mark or change identity, to make or foster community, to heal, to teach, persuade, or convince, and to deal with the sacred or demonic.[55]

Relatedly, the third theme to come from the Rosa skatepark interviews is the social effect of the skatepark – in terms of helping 'both girls and boys develop their personalities'[56] through interactions with each other and with 'foreigners' (SkatePal volunteers). A local man who visits the skatepark on a regular basis, 'K', explained that since the skatepark has been built he has noticed a change in the attitudes of young people who use the park. He explained,

> I ask the headmasters of the school, the teachers, about the kids, and they say that it's a really amazing thing. You know the kids started to change. … All the kids, they come, they started to express themselves much better than before. They are more open than before. They are stronger than before, and they are willing to do lots of things like voluntary things – towards the school and towards each other. This is something very interesting, that comes from the skatepark.[57]

When I asked K about his hopes for the future of skateboarding in Palestine, he said he hoped that more skateparks could be built in Palestine, 'Not just [for] kids, even adults. They deserve something. A place where they can really show themselves. Not just for other people, but for themselves, physically'. For clarification, I asked whether K's comment about 'showing themselves' meant 'expressing themselves', and he continued,

> Exactly. Because here [in the skatepark], you can decide your strategy for your life, for one day, without thinking about permissions from the Israeli authorities, without thinking about checkpoints, without thinking about incursions and other things. … That's the really devastating thing. Destroying themselves from inside. Of course when you think of teenagers, they would always like to show themselves up. They want to show themselves that they can do something… on a minimum base when they have this skatepark they go and they know how to move and jump, and how to go on a skateboard, showing people. That people are focusing on them gives them the feeling that they are doing something good, and people really admiring you.

In the context of the West Bank, K's conception of self-expression is understood to represent freedom of thought and action, and the ability for people

98 *'Skateboard philanthropy'*

to contribute actively to a public arena that is beyond the realms of the home, of work, and of functional activity. Skateboarding offers an outlet for a public performance of self that is recognised as an important part of social and personal life.

Generosity – of deed and thought

SkatePal's construction of the skatepark in Asira involved around 20 volunteers – all of whom were skateboarders. The group included myself and one other woman volunteer. When we were building the skatepark the presence of us – two women working on the site – was considered strange to most local people, and to some it was inappropriate work for us to be doing. From the beginning of the process, complexities around gender have been embedded in the project. A local man who had offered us much help and support would often suggest that we might spend the day with him and his family rather than continue working. On several occasions in what I understood as an act of chivalry, young men from the town would insist on taking equipment from me and to do the work themselves.

Our presence also initiated generous acts of solidarity. On one occasion, a woman visited the site with her husband. After watching me move breeze blocks from one part of the site to another, the woman came over and began helping me for a short while before she and her husband went away. A group of boys – around the ages of 10 to 15 would often cycle up to the building site to watch us. One day, towards the end of the build, the boys had come to visit and were sat close to me as we exchanged words and joked. After a while, one of the boys looked at me inquisitively – as if he was working something out – and said, in a curious way, 'you are just like a man'. Showing an understanding of gender complexity, he recognised that I was a woman behaving in a way typically defined as masculine.

As has already been mentioned in this chapter, we initiated skateboarding practice with girls at one of the local girl's schools before the skatepark was built with the hope that we could establish skateboarding as an activity for all. On my second visit to the skatepark, the following year after it had been built, I observed that very few of the girls we had worked with during the skatepark build were using the skatepark. I made some enquiries with local people who suggested the problem was that the skatepark does not have girls-only sessions. This was confirmed in more detail in my conversation with the headteacher of the girl's school.[58] For most families, separate sessions for girls and boys were preferred. This is not to say that no girls use the park – SkatePal have around 40% women and girls participation at the Asira skatepark. They tend to be girls below the age of puberty, who are not yet subject to socially prescribed separation between young

'Skateboard philanthropy' 99

men and women. SkatePal have consistently sought to operate in a way that recognises the needs of the local community and have been working with their local partners to find ways of initiating girls- and women-only time in the skatepark. This necessitates additional layers of commitment and organisation that require funding and municipal support to ensure that the skatepark, which is publicly open and free to use, can sustain girls-only time that is sufficiently respected by young men and boys in the community.

The problem of creating space for girls and women has resource implications and it is not only a social and cultural issue, it also requires a modified perspective on inclusivity. When I visited the Asira skatepark annually, I met with several SkatePal volunteers who I asked about the participation of women and girls. In most cases their perception was that the skatepark operates as an inclusive gendered space, as evidenced by the presence of girls using the park and the welcoming and supportive environment fostered by volunteers and local people. These are, of course, laudable and important things. My research suggests that within skateboarding philanthropy projects there is a need to be more generous in thought and action, by considering who isn't there, who can't visit the skatepark, and to explore the barriers to entry that aren't always patently obvious.

Conclusion

In the open framework set up by SkatePal, participants are given the freedom to explore and experiment with bodily movement, which elicited responses in participants and observers that suggests the development of a broad range of physical skills and self-expression. These interviews also contain a considerable emphasis on the transferability of skills and learning experiences from skateboarding to other activities and aspects of life. These claims are not measurable, but these kinds of statements do stand as a clear indication of the perception of skateboarding as a worthwhile and enriching activity.

In skateboarding philanthropy projects, this kind of open self-learning is sometimes paired with more instrumentalist learning, such as can be seen in the cases of Skateistan and in SkateQilya. The first international skateboarding development initiative, Skateistan, which was founded by Oliver Percovich began in Afghanistan and then branched out to the delivery of projects in South Africa and Cambodia. As Thorpe explains, Skateistan utilises skateboarding 'as a carrot';[59] the activity draws interest and participation from children who are then entered into taught art and language education within Skateistan facilities. Similarly, SkateQilya, a skateboarding NGO that, like SkatePal, operates within the West Bank and is headed by Mohammed Othman began by integrating skateboarding with teaching

100 *'Skateboard philanthropy'*

children and young people photography, video skills, community building and leadership training and has developed to include conversational English classes and social media training.[60] Whilst these skills are important and highly relevant to the communities in which Skateistan and SkateQilya work, it is also important to recognise the somatic practice and learning that occurs through more open and unstructured movement.

In the example of Rosa skatepark, the observations and findings I discovered are most interesting when they are positioned against an understanding of the local social framework. Skateboarding philanthropy in the case of SkatePal operates through a discourse of generosity through self-conduct and relationship to others, a willingness to embrace bodily knowing wholeheartedly, expressions of public movement creativity, and in thinking and responding generously to social and cultural differences of practice.

Notes

1 Simon Darnell, (2012), 'Situating Sport-for-Development and the "Sport for Development and Peace" Sector' in S. Darnell, (ed.), *Sport for Development and Peace: A Critical Sociology*, Bloomsbury Academic, London, 1–21.

2 Ibid.; Belinda Wheaton, Georgina Roy, and Rebecca Olive, (2017), 'Exploring Critical Alternatives for Youth Development Through Lifestyle Sport: Surfing and Community Development in Aotearoa/New Zealand', *Sustainability*, 9(12), 2298–2343; Holly Thorpe, (2016), 'Action Sports for Youth Development: Critical Insights for the SDP Community', *International Journal of Sport Policy and Politics*, 8(1), 91–116; Holly Thorpe and Nida Ahmad, (2015), 'Youth, Action Sports and Political Agency in the Middle East: Lessons from a Grassroots Parkour Group in Gaza', *Sociology of Sport*, 50(6), 678–704; Sophie Friedel, (2015), *The Art of Living Sideways: Skateboarding, Peace and Elicitive Conflict Transformation*, Springer, New York; Holly Thorpe and Robert Rinehart, (2013), 'Action Sports NGOs in a Neo-Liberal Context: The Cases of Skateistan and Surf Aid International', *Journal of Sport and Social Issues*, 37(2), 115–141; Simon Darnell, (2010), 'Power, Politics and "Sport for Development and Peace": Investigating the Utility of Sport for International Development', *Sociology of Sport Journal*, 27, 54–75; Martha Saavedra, (2009), 'Dilemmas and Opportunities in Gender and Sport-in-Development' in R. Levermore and A. Beacom, (eds.), *Sport and International Development*, Palgrave Macmillan, London, 124–155.

3 Paul O'Connor, (2016), 'Skateboard Philanthropy: Inclusion and Prefigurative Politics' in K.-J. Lombard, (ed.), *Skateboarding: Subcultures, Sites and Shifts*, Routledge, London/New York, 30–43.

4 Thorpe.

5 Thorpe, 101.

6 Wheaton, Roy, and Olive.

7 Tony Hawk, (2018), 'Thoughts on Olympic Skateboarding', *Medium*, Oct 9. Available at https://medium.com/s/story/skateboarding-will-be-in-the-olympics-in-less-than-two-years-4bdcb8734061 (Accessed 8 July 2019); Matt Beare, (2017), 'The Daily Push – Skateboarding as Sport: Why Our Bodies Hurt', *The Berrics*, Oct 4. Available at https://theberrics.com/the-daily-push-is-skateboar

'*Skateboard philanthropy*' 101

ding-a-sport (Accessed 8 July 2019); Johnathan Russell Clarke, (2016), 'With Skateboarding Headed to the Olympics, What's Next for the Anti-Sport?', *Rolling Stone*, Aug 25. Available at https://www.rollingstone.com/culture/culture-sports/with-skateboarding-heading-to-the-olympics-whats-next-for-the-anti-sport-248563/ (Accessed 8 July 2019); David Wharton, (2015), 'Some Skateboarders Want No Part of the Olympics', *Los Angeles Times*, Oct 12. Available at https://www.latimes.com/sports/sportsnow/la-sp-sn-skateboarders-no-olympics-20151012-story.html (Accessed 8 July 2019).

8 Saavedra.
9 Darnell, (2012).
10 Helen Thomas, (ed.), (1993), *Dance, Gender and Culture*, Macmillan, London.
11 Roger Copeland, (1993), 'Dance, Feminism and the Critique of the Visual' in H. Thomas, (ed.), *Dance, Gender and Culture*, Macmillan, London, 139–150.
12 Christine Caldwell and Lucy Leighton, (2016), 'Dance/Movement Therapy, Women's Rights, and Feminism: The First 50 Years', *American Dance Therapy Association*, 38, 279–284.
13 Ibid., 282.
14 O'Connor.
15 Ibid., 40.
16 Ibid.
17 R [anonymised respondent], (2018), Interview, September.
18 Dana Mills, (2017), 'The Beat Goes On: The Story of Palestine's National Dance', *+972*. Available at https://972mag.com/the-beat-goes-on-the-story-of-palestines-national-dance/129789/ (Accessed 17 July 2019).
19 AR [anonymised respondent], (2018), Interview, September.
20 Headteacher of girl's school, (2018), Interview, September.
21 Ibid.
22 Kelly Jean Mullan, (2014), 'Somatics: Investigating the Common Ground of Western Body-Mind Disciplines', *Body, Movement and Dance in Psychotherapy*, 9(4), 253–265.
23 Martha Eddy, (2009), 'A Brief History of Somatic Practices and Dance: Historical Development of the Field of Somatic Education and Its Relationship to Dance', *Journal of Dance and Somatic Practices*, 1(1), 5–27.
24 Jill Green, (2002), 'Somatic Knowledge: The Body as Content and Methodology in Dance Education', *Journal of Dance Education*, 2(4), 114–118.
25 Mullan, 253.
26 Eddy.
27 Green, 116.
28 Martha Eddy, (2002), 'Somatic Practices and Dance: Global Influences', *Dance Research Journal*, 34(2), 46–62.
29 Friedel.
30 Ibid., 93.
31 Sophie Friedel, (n.d.), 'Drop In Ride Out: Therapeutic Skateboard and Drive Longboard', *Rollbrett Workshop*. Available at https://www.rollbrettworkshop.org/dropinrideout (Accessed 19 July 2019).
32 Gary Yontef, (1993), 'Gestalt Therapy: An Introduction', *Awareness, Dialogue and Process*, The Gestalt Journal Press. Available at https://www.gestalt.org/yontef.htm (Accessed 19 July 2019).
33 The A.skate Foundation, (n.d.), 'About A.skate', *A.skate Foundation*. Available at http://www.askate.org/about_askate (Accessed 19 July 2019).

102 *'Skateboard philanthropy'*

34 Emily Wang in Matt Allen, (2018), 'Push to Heal', *Vimeo*. Available at https://vimeo.com/281117753 (Accessed 20 July 2019).

35 Graham Bradley, (2010), 'Skate Parks as a Context for Adolescent Development', *Journal of Adolescent Research*, 25(2), 288–323.

36 S [anonymised respondent], (2018), Interview, September.

37 A [anonymised respondent], (2018), Interview, September.

38 Peter Whitley and Alec Beck in Tony Hawk Foundation, (2018), 'Skateboarding as Emotional Therapy' [podcast], *Tony Hawk Foundation*, Feb 23. Available at https://tonyhawkfoundation.org/2018/02/episode-15-skateboarding-as-emotional-therapy/ (Accessed 20 July 2019).

39 Åsa Bäckström, (2014), 'Knowing and Teaching Kineasthetic Experience in Skateboarding: An Example of Sensory Emplacement', *Sport, Education and Society*, 19(6), 752–772.

40 Ibid., 765.

41 Whitley and Beck.

42 Dani Abulhawa, (2017), 'Smoothing Space in Palestine: Building a Skatepark and a Socio-Political Forum with the SkatePal Charity', *Journal of Urban Cultural Studies*, 4(3), 417–426.

43 J [anonymised respondent], (2018), Interview, September.

44 David Buckingham, (2009), 'Skate Perception: Self-Representation, Identity and Visual Style in a Youth Subculture' in D. Buckingham and R. Willet, (eds.), *Video Cultures: Media Technology and Everyday Creativity*, Palgrave Macmillan, Basingstoke and New York, 133–151, p. 140.

45 Sidewalk Magazine, (2013), 'Click Bait 2013: The Year in Review – Part 2', *Sidewalk Magazine*. Available at https://sidewalkmag.com/skateboard-news/click-bait-2013-the-year-in-review-part-2.html/6 (Accessed 24 July 2019).

46 Offthewalltv, (2012), 'Grosso's Loveletters to Skateboarding – Style', *YouTube*, Sep 4. Available at https://www.youtube.com/watch?v=rGOA5Yv1xVk (Accessed 25 July 2019).

47 John Cardiel, ibid.

48 Jason Dill, ibid.

49 Greg Hunt, ibid.

50 Cardiel, ibid.

51 Dwayne Peters, ibid.

52 Jane Bacon, (2012), 'Her Body Finds a Voice: Authentic Movement in an Imaginal World', *Body, Movement and Dance in Psychotherapy*, 7(2), 115–127.

53 Eddy.

54 Marie Forgeard and James Kaufman, (2016), 'Who Cares About Imagination, Creativity and Innovation, and Why? A Review', *Psychology of Aesthetics, Creativity, and the Arts*, 10(3), 250–269.

55 Richard Schechner, (2002), *Performance Studies: An Introduction*, Routledge, London/New York.

56 A [anonymised respondent].

57 K [anonymised respondent], (2017), Interview, September.

58 Headteacher of girl's school.

59 Thorpe, (2016).

60 Adam Abel Studio, (2017), 'SkateQilya 2017 Summer Camp Trailer', *Vimeo*. Available at https://vimeo.com/221264176 (Accessed 11 July 2019).

Conclusion
Skateboarding's participation in the world beyond itself

On a sunny afternoon in Manchester I went with a friend to Platt Fields's skatepark. A series of tired wooden ramps and fun boxes always in need of re-surfacing that sit on a smooth-ish rectangle of concrete. When we arrived on this day, there were quite a few boys aged between 12 and 16 using the park on their skateboards, scooters, and BMXs. Towards the end of their session, two of the skateboarders were stood near me at the top of one of the smaller quarter pipes. One of the boys looked over at a car pulling into the nearby carpark, turned to his friend stood next to him and said 'hey, your bitch is here'. On hearing this I reacted almost involuntarily, saying, 'don't talk about a woman like that'. 'It's a joke', he said. My friend, overhearing this too, cut across us to reply to the boy, 'it doesn't matter. It's not appropriate'. We could tell the boy wasn't used to being talked back to, and not here in a place that he felt he belonged to and that belonged to him.

Skateparks – like any public gathering place – are sites of social forum in which views and perspectives are expressed and challenged. As skateboarding has grown older and more diverse, the presence of such a varied range of participants brings different dynamics to the culture. This includes a wide range of people who aren't going to sit back and allow misogynist, homophobic, and racist language and actions to go unchallenged. Importantly, this work is not only happening at the micro level of skateboarder-to-skateboarder interactions described above. In 2013, professional skateboarder Nyjah Huston made a comment about women skateboarders that was published in a *Thrasher* magazine interview. Huston is a professional skateboarder who has won seven X Games gold medals, and numerous Street League competitions, including the Super Crown in 2017 and 2014. He is sponsored by Element, Monster Energy, and Nike amongst others, and has won more prize money through competitions than any other skateboarder in history. Huston is a highly consistent competitive skateboarder, and one who is generally representative of the more commercial and competitive side of skateboarding culture, rather than the 'outlaw' spirit of what has generally

104 *Conclusion*

been regarded as 'core'. The interview between Huston and late *Thrasher* editor Jake Phelps began with a discussion about restrictive skatepark rules, 'jock dads' and kids who love the X Games, which can be read as a jibe towards Huston's relationship to the corporate, safe, and competitive side of skateboarding, as well as his history of coaching by his strict and controlling father.[1] The interview then turned to a discussion of women skateboarders after Phelps asserted that skateboarding 'ain't for pussies', and he oriented the conversation to talk about a downhill contest he watched where he saw a girl get badly hurt. The conversation went as follows:

Phelps: We went to this downhill contest last week and I saw this girl get served up so hard.
Huston: Why was a girl skating a downhill contest?
Phelps: The women do downhill stuff because they think it's like sidewalk surfing. They don't realise how dangerous it really is.
Huston: You could get way more served up skating downhill than you could skating a ten-stair rail. Some girls can skate but I personally believe that skateboarding is not for girls at all. Not one bit.
Phelps: That one girl did a 540, but that's vert.
Huston: Yeah street skating is completely different.[2]

When the magazine was published, Huston's comment that 'girls shouldn't skate at all' became a highlighted pull quote, which was met with much criticism and commentary on social media channels and prompted a formal apology from the 19-year-old a few days later.[3] Some commenters also highlighted the complicity of Phelps in the production of Huston's comments. Anthony Pappalardo wrote,

> Throughout the issue there's plenty to take issue with if you're looking for potentially sexist, racist, or homophobic stuff. Jamie Tancowny talks about everyone getting 'beaver fever' on tour, Leo Romero recalls people tripping out because a man kissed him at a signing (it was his dad), James Hardy is asked about his 'girl cars'… and Al Davis is asked why his name is Alex and if he's been to jail because he's black. No one is buzzing about any of those interviews though.[4]

Whilst not intending to defend Huston, Pappalardo's article questions a culture of immunity around Phelps and *Thrasher* and why it is that Huston is so comfortably framed as villain. In Pappalardo's view, Huston represents the commercialisation of skateboarding and is extremely successful, which makes him a popular target for criticism.

Conclusion 105

The Phelps-Huston interview reads as an example of masculine domination, following Raewyn Connell and James Messerschmidt's rethinking of hegemonic masculinity, in which they explain, '"masculinity" represents not a certain type of man but, rather, a way that men position themselves through discursive practices'.[5] Phelps is the arbiter of skateboarding as a subcultural, tough, outlaw, exclusionary form of skateboarding that is simply 'not for "pussies"'. Huston's own practice does not quite fit into this framing, but their opinions are able to find convergence through a shared regulation of womens bodies. The fact that the structures which produce and maintain this kind of discrimination are being illuminated by commentators at the populist level evidences a considerable shift in skateboarding culture. From a structural perspective, Phelps set the tone of the piece by reminiscing over skateboarding's 'outlaw' past, admonishing the increasingly safe/sanctioned spaces of skateparks, and highlighting how tough skateboarders have to be. Phelps suggests that women downhill skateboarders do not understand what they are doing and fails to register the name of the 'one girl' who did a 540, as well as disqualifying its relevance because it was performed on vert. In response, Girl Skate Network published a blog post where they wrote, '"that one girl" that did a 540 is actually two and their names are Lyn-z Adams Hawkins Pastrana and Alana Smith'.[6]

The analysis within this book has pointed to skateboarding's current socio-political moment of critical self-reflexivity, which is evidenced by the increased range of criticism of skateboarders and skateboarding culture that has been expressed in populist skateboarding media sources over the past five years.[7] This has, in part, been enabled by the democratising power of the Internet and the availability of a broader range of media platforms that are willing to publish content challenging the status quo of the industry and of the perspectives of influential persons. In 2018, skateboarder, writer, and academic Kyle Beachy struggled to publish his article, 'Primitive Progressivism', a piece that holds to account former professional skateboarder Jason Jessee's racist and homophobic comments and, in a similar manner to Pappalardo's example above, spotlights a skateboarding industry framework that allowed Jessee's attitudes to go unchallenged. The article was eventually published by *Free Skateboard Magazine*. In it Beachy asks,

is skateboarding a primitive force, or is it a progressive one? Or more than that: will skateboarding continue to perpetuate the old American power dynamics of few and many, of white supremacy and brown otherness, or will it work to dismantle them? Does it PMA its way into cozy selfishness or play a more difficult and labor-intensive role in the world beyond itself?[8]

106   *Conclusion*

These questions can be applied across a range of issues, especially ones relating to gender equity and feminal support. There has been a historic tendency in skateboarding for critique of any kind to be quashed under the suggestion that skateboarding has an intrinsic innocence and can be excluded from social and political critique, which is encapsulated by comments along the lines of, 'shut up and skate'. The sentiment that skateboarders might occupy the 'Holden Caulfield' position of a perpetual idealised ignorance to social power structures and privilege is unsustainable. As Beachy's quote suggests, skateboarding is on the brink of these questions: to perpetuate or deconstruct asymmetries of power? To move towards insularity or towards participation in the world beyond itself?

This book has offered something in response to these questions; namely, why it might be so important to deconstruct skateboarding cultural practices and participate in the world, and how this can be done. It is easy to overlook skateboarding – at its essence it is a form of playing; an activity generally seen as lacking in value beyond itself. Much more than 'just playing', the physical culture of skateboarding reveals a symbolism inherent in specific tricks and skateboarding movement that carries meanings and feelings, not only for us as skateboarders, but for observers of skateboarding as well. Moving your body in certain ways has an effect on the body that performs, but as a publicly performed activity it also operates within the social-spatial realm and has an effect on the person or people that witness movement in space at a particular moment of time.

Skateboarding practice is marked by bodily movement and routes to bodily sensations that are frequently likened to gliding, to cheating physics, and to flying. The skateboard offers participants a freedom of movement that goes beyond the possibilities of the body, and with such a broad range of movement that the possibilities of tricks and combinations performed on different obstacles and terrain are seemingly endless. The practice of specific skateboarders highlights the ways that a person's somatic heritage[9] informs the innovation and development of their own style and technique.

Women who skateboard equally contribute to this culture and they enact a challenge against women's historical restriction of bodily comportment through their approach to movement and occupation of space in the world. In a selection of essays, Iris Marion Young articulates how girls and women are socially encouraged to be fearful of harm to their bodies, to distrust their physical capabilities, and she examines how women tend to occupy space in a far more restricted way than men do.[10] In her work, Young also explores the performativity of restriction; a process by which social frameworks in which women are more physically restricted than men perpetuate an association of femininity with fragility and physical inhibition that becomes seen as natural or intrinsic to people who identify as feminal. Performances of

Conclusion 107

restriction, she writes, 'produce in many women a greater or lesser feeling of incapacity, frustration and self-consciousness. We have more of a tendency than men do to greatly underestimate our bodily capacity'.[11] Activities, such as that of skateboarding, which encourage physical activity, extraordinary bodily comportment, and detailed bodily and movement understanding, are not only important to maintaining active lifestyles, but also in raising the importance of creative self-expression, which is a vital part of human functioning and well-being at the personal, community, and social levels. Supporting the increased physical activity and bodily comportment of girls and women also goes some way toward re-visioning femininity, as a gender identity associated with strength and physical freedom.

Young's essays were originally published in the 1970s and 1980s, but with their re-publication in 2005 the inequalities she highlights are still relevant today. In a 2018 Lancet report on global health including 168 countries, data collected during 2016 showed that more than a quarter of adults globally do not get enough physical activity. Within this data, researchers identified a clear gender gap with a difference of at least 10% between men and women in 65 countries, and a difference of at least 20% in nine countries.[12] The findings from this research suggest a need to examine the ways in which women and girls feel excluded from or lack the confidence to engage in all forms of physical activity. My hope is that the ideas explored within this book can serve to offer something towards this endeavour within the realm of skateboarding practice, and to offer a historical lineage and discursive support for widened participation in skateboarding from people who identify beyond skateboarding's typical masculinity.

There are many sports and creative activities that people can take part in, which is important because not everyone is drawn to or can thrive within the same kinds of movement and social-spatial matrices. Skateboarding is understood as an activity in which participants are 'intrinsically motivated' rather than being motivated through regulatory frameworks such as coaching, systemised practice, or specified technique.[13] In this way, skateboarding appeals to people who, in some cases, do not wish to participate in traditional sports or dance, or who lack interest in or have little opportunity to engage in other sorts of creative practice. Raising the value of skateboarding as a form of physical activity for people of any gender is also of great importance.

The freedom of self-defined learning, progression, and development that is so much a part of skateboarding has also contributed to philanthropic projects in which skateboarding charities are able to avoid disempowering communities by leaving a lot of room for individuals to take up skateboarding in a way that allows them to understand and display their own authentic individualism.

108 *Conclusion*

This book has also highlighted the importance of allies in which people who hold power actively work to open up spaces of belonging for others. The creation of cultures that support the participation of many are ones that can sustain themselves over time and that can build powerful social bonds between people from sometimes vastly different backgrounds and with a range of different life experiences. Critical voices for change and development have come together in recent years. What we are advocating for is radical openness, inclusivity, and generosity from one skateboarder to another, within the skateboarding industry, and within broader social and academic structures to value and support femininity.

Notes

1 Kyle Beachy, (2011), 'You're Not Me: Nyjah Huston and Inflationary Spectacle', *The Classical*, Dec 8. Available at http://theclassical.org/articles/youre-not-me -nyjah-huston-and-inflationary-spectacle (Accessed 25 September 2019); ESPN UK, (2013), 'Nyjah Huston: Growing Pains,' *YouTube*, Jun 28. Available at https ://www.youtube.com/watch?v=keESOFr64Gk (Accessed 25 September 2019).
2 Jake Phelps and Nyjah Huston, (2013), 'The Interview Issue: Huston', *Thrasher*, July, 165–177, 177.
3 Colin Bane, (2013), 'Huston Sorry for Comments About Female Skaters', *X -Games.com*, Jun 4. Available at http://www.xgames.com/skateboarding/article /9342843/nyjah-huston-apologizes-comments-female-skateboarders (Accessed 30 September 2019).
4 Anthony Pappalardo, (2013), 'Thoughts on Nyjah Huston's Comment: "Skateboarding Is Not for Firls"', *Jenkem*, June 10. Available at http://www .jenkemmag.com/home/2013/06/10/thoughts-on-nyjah-hustons-comment-skate boarding-is-not-for-girls/ (Accessed 25 September 2019).
5 Raewyn Connell and James Messerschmidt, (2005), 'Hegemonic Masculinity: Rethinking the Concept', *Gender and Society*, 19, 829–859, 841.
6 Girl Skate Network, (2013), 'Skateboarding Is Not for Girls,' *Girl Skate Network Blog*, June 2. Available at http://girlsskatenetwork.com/2013/06/02/skateboard ing-is-not-for-girls/ (Accessed 25 September 2019).
7 Linnea Bullion, (2018), 'My Experiences in Skateboarding', *Jenkem*, Aug 21. Available at http://www.jenkemmag.com/home/2018/08/21/my-experiences-in -skateboarding/ (Accessed 25 September 2019); Kyle Beachy, (2018), 'Primitive Progressivism', *Free Skateboard Magazine*, June 5. Available at https://ww w.freeskatemag.com/2018/06/05/primitive-progressivism-by-kyle-beachy/ (Accessed 25 September 2019); Jonathan Smith, (2014), 'Maybe We Shouldn't Be So Quick to Idolize a Gay-Bashing Skateboarder', *Vice*, Aug 19. Available at https://www.vice.com/en_us/article/jmbbk3/maybe-we-shouldnt-be-so-sent imental-about-a-gay-bashing-skateboarder-658 (Accessed 25 September 2019).
8 Beachy, (2018), n.p.
9 Elizabeth Dempster, (2008), 'The Choreography of the Pedestrian', *Performance Research*, 13(1), 23–28.
10 Iris Marion Young, (2005), *On Female Body Experience: 'Throwing Like a Girl' and Other Essays*, Oxford University Press, New York.

Conclusion 109

11 Ibid., 34.
12 Regina Guthold, Gretchen A. Stephens, Leanne M. Riley, and Fiona C. Bull, (2018), 'Worldwide Trends in Insufficient Physical Activity from 2001 to 2016: A Pooled Analysis of 358 Population-Based Surveys with 1 9 Million Participants', *The Lancet Global Health*, 6(10), 1077–1086. Available at https://doi.org/10.1016/S2214-109X(18)30357-7 (Accessed 30 September 2019).
13 Tim Seifert and C. Hedderson, (2010), 'Intrinsic Motivation and Flow in Skateboarding: An Ethnographic Study', *Journal of Happiness Studies*, 11, 277–292, 279.

Index

Note: Page numbers in *italics* indicate figures.

Aapola, Sinikka 7
Adams, Lucy 30, *30*, 47
Ahmed, Sara 56
Akkerman, Abraham 74
Alibo, Sandy 34
Alice (character) 6–8
Alice's Adventures in Wonderland (Carroll) 6–7
Ali Khan, Carolyn 1
alternative skateboarding culture 26, 33–34, 37–38
Alva, Tony 24, 71
Armanto, Lizzie 53
As If, And What? 33
Asira Al-Shamalyia 4, 82, 84–86; *see also* Rosa skatepark (Asira Al-Shamalyia)
A.skate Foundation 90
Atencio, Matthew 10, 68
authentic individualism 51–52, 54, 71, 107
Authentic Movement 87

Babe's Brigade 34
Bacha Posh 8
Bäckström, Åsa 3, 92
backyard skateboarding 18, 22, 65
Bahne team 19
Baker, Leo: authentic individualism and 52; collective support and 52; critique of masculinist skateboarding industry 45–46, 50, 56; feminist stance and 12, 51; interviews with 53; on the male gaze 50–51;

personal style and 50–51; separatism and 46; skateboard design and 49–50; support for women and queer skateboarders 45
Bakhtin, Mikhail 7
Baltimore, Megan 27–28
Barker, Thomas 11
Barrow, Ted 55–56
Bastomski, Sara 74
Bates, Sevie 24
Battieste, Stephanie 34
Baumgardner, Jennifer 35
Beachy, Kyle 105–106
Beal, Becky 2, 10, 23, 68
Beck, Alec 91
Bemiller, Michelle L. 56
Berrics, The 52
Berryman, Cindy 18
Berryman, Ellen 18
Big Brother 26–27, 55
Birdhouse Skateboards 71
Black, Noel 16
Blind Skateboard 66
Blouin, Bonnie 23
Blumenfeld-Jones, Donald 72–73
bodily-kinaesthetic intelligence 72–73, 75, 77
Body Issue (ESPN) 52–53
Bolster, Warren 21
Bondi, Liz 74
Bones Brigade 20, 22, 71
Borden, Iain 2, 18–19, 26
Botwid, Tom 10
Bradley, Graham L. 90

Index 111

Brevard, Samarria 53
Broadly (Vice) 32, 45, 50
Brooke, Michael 2, 23
Brown, David 63
Brujas 44
Buckingham, David 94–95
Bufoni, Leticia 12, 29, 52–54, 56
Burke, Carolyn 7–8
Burnside, Cara-Beth 23, 29
BUST magazine 24
Butz, Konstantin 37

Caldwell, Christine 83
Cardiel, John 95
Carr, John 74–75
Carroll, Lewis 6–8
Carroll, Mike 27
Carving Space 34
Catcher in the Rye, The (Salinger) 10
Caulfield, Holden (character) 10
Cespedes, Kim 18
Cheers Skateboards 29
Child Trauma Academy 90
Cixous, Hélène 6
Clark, Saecha 26
Clueless 63
Cobain, Kurt 63
Cold War 67
Cole, Louison 45
communities of practice 49, 74–77
Concrete Wave 23
Connell, Raewyn 105
Cooler Magazine 52–53
Copeland, Roger 83
core identity 9, 11–12, 27, 55, 64, 71
creative self-expression 94–97, 107
Crenshaw, Kimberlé 37
critical race theory 37
Crum, Maddie 25
Currie, Dawn 51–52

Dabbadie, M. 38
Dabke dancing 86
Dal Santo, Marisa 55, 69
dance 73, 82–83, 86–87, 95
dance and movement therapy
 (DMT) 83
Darnell, Simon 81
Davis, Al 104
Davis, Charlie 86

Davis, James 2
Dean-Ganek, Annie 34
Dee, Aurora 68, 70
Devil's Toy, The 18, 20
Devrim Zamani board 31, *32*
Dill, Jason 95
Dixon, Dwayne 8
Dogtown and Z-Boys 9, 20, 36, 65–66
downhill racing 9, 62, 104–105
Doyenne 38
Driscoll, Catherine 25
drop in 92–93, *93*
Drop In Ride Out programme 89
Dumas, Alex 68
Duncan, Isadora 87

Ebeling, Kristin 34
Eddy, Martha 87
Edelman, Marian Wright 33
Eisenhour, Mackenzie 53, 71
Ensler, Eve 9
#Equality campaign 49
Equal Time 24, 28

Falbo, Mario 47
Feldenkrais Method 87
feminal skateboarders: authentic
 individualism and 51–52, 54; defined
 5; feminist politics and 45–46,
 57; gender regulation and 52–56;
 male gaze and 49–52; personal
 responsibility and 53–54; personal
 style and 50–51; as role models
 50–51; separatism and 45–49; space-
 making by 49, 57; technique and 73;
 see also women skateboarders
femininity 5, 16, 52, 63–64, 73
feminism: authentic individualism
 and 51–52; critical race 37; dance
 and 83; economic equality and 44;
 girl-ness and 25; intersectional 44;
 polyphonus 57; post-feminist 58;
 self-owned objectification and 25;
 understandings of 44–45; unified 37;
 waves of 57; women skateboarders
 and 44–45, 51
feminist politics: feminal skateboarders
 and 45–49, 57; gender regulation
 and 52–56; male gaze and 49–52;
 normalisation of sexism and 48;

112   Index

post-structuralist 51, 57; separatism and 45–49
Fine, Hunter 3, 22
flatland tricks 19, 62
Forgeard, Marie 96
Foucault, Michel 57
Francombe-Webb, Jessica 38
Free Skateboard Magazine 105
freestyle skateboarding: derisory place of 19; development of tricks in 20; early skateboarding and 9, 66; physical styles of 67; unusual objects in 63; women and 23
Friedel, Sophie 3, 84, 88–90

Garber-Paul, Elizabeth 49
Gardner, Howard 72
Garrick, Marnina 7
Gaudio, Matt 29
gender centering 64
gender identity 1, 5, 45, 62–64
gender non-binary skateboarders 33–34, 37, 46
genderqueer skateboarders 37–38
gender regulation 52–56, 105
gestalt therapy 89
Gibb, Olivia 63
Gil, Arianna 44
girl/girlhood: Alice (character) 6–8; Bacha Posh 8; defining 24–25, 35; derogatory use of term 25, 29; feminine archetypes and 6; as a gendered concept 6, 9; hysteria and 7; making space for 99; marketing discourse and 24, 30–31; multiplicity and 7–8; Ophelia (character) 6–8; as powerful state of becoming 7–8
Girl is NOT a 4 Letter Word 29, 32, 44, 53
girl power 25
Girl Riders Org 34
Girl Skate Alliance 32
Girl Skate Australia 34
Girl Skateboards 27–28
Girl Skate India 34
Girl Skate Network 32, 105
Girl Skate UK 34, 52
Glapka, Ewa 51
Göggel, Sabrina 29
Gonzalez, Mark 10, 65–66

Graham, Martha 87
Green, Ben 71
Green, Jill 87
Grosso, Jeff 95

Haddad, Sam 10, 52
Hags, The 24
Hamlet (Shakespeare) 6
Haraway, Donna 37
Hardy, James 104
Harris, Anita 7
Harrison-Caldwell, Max 11
Hawk, Tony 70–72, 76–77
hegemonic masculinity 105
Heller, Rebecca 2, 24
Highsnobiety 76
hill bombing 62
History of Women in Skateboarding, The (Porter) 2
Hoefler, Kelvin 29
Hoopla Skateboards 29
Hosoi, Christian 71
Howard, Rick 27
Huck 23, 37, 66
Hull Services 90
Hunt, Greg 95
Huston, Nyjah 103–105

Ianucci, Gino 95
International Association for Skateboard Companies 11
intersectional feminism 44
Irigaray, Luce 7–8

Jaks, The 24
Jarvis, Helen 74
Jenkem 28, 69
Jerusalem Skater Girls 44
Jessee, Jason 105
Johnson, Lesley 7–8
Johnston, Lynda 1
Jonze, Spike 27
Jutra, Claude 18

Kaufman, James 96
Kelly, Deirdre 51–52
Kinney, Abbot 65
Kliewer, Jan 10
Knoop, Mimi 29
Komaromi, Teigan *33*

Index 113

Kramer, Lynn 24, 28
Kurland, Andrea 66

Laban, Rudolf 87
Laforest, Sophie 68
Leighton, Lucy 83
Liao, Jilleen 28, 46–48
Liddell, Alice 8
Logan, Robin 18
Lombard, Kara-Jane 62
longboarding 35
Long Live Southbank 83
Lovenskate 30–31

Mahfia 32
male gaze 49–52
Markula, Pirkko 38
masculinity: alternative forms of 1;
   bodily-kinaesthetic intelligence and
   73; core skateboarding identity and
   9, 11–12, 27, 55, 64, 71; gender
   presentations and 1; hegemonic
   105; physical culture and 69–70,
   73, 76; skateboarding culture and
   19, 51; skateboarding industry and
   45–46, 50; sporting activities and 73;
   stoicism and 69–70, 77; transcending
   bodily limits and 69–70
Massey, Doreen 74
McClain, ZáNean 10
McConnell-Ginet, Sally 25
McCormack, Karen 48
McGee, Patti 16–17
McKee, Marc 25
Mearns, Drew 29
Medlock, Laura 24
Menke, Louisa 47
Men's Health Brazil 52
Meow Skateboards 29, 32, 49
Meow Skateboards (2014) 45
Messerschmidt, James 105
methodology 3–5
Meurle, Sarah 10
Mills, Sara 57
Monster Children 10
Moore, Joe 63, *64*
Mortimer, Sean 2
Moselle, Crystal 24
Mountain, Lance 17, 66
mountain biking 48

movement: decisiveness and 92–93;
   drop in 92–93, *93*; expressions of
   13; ollie 91–92, *92*; pushing and
   91, *92*; skateboarder cues from
   96; skateboarding culture and
   12–13, 91–92, 106; symbolic 91–93;
   unstructured 100
Moving Boarders (Atencio et. al) 10
Mullen, Rodney 20
Mulvey, Laura 51
My World 45

National Action Sports Show
   (NASS) 33
Nefarious Crew 44
Neurosequential Model of Therapeutics
   (NMT) 90
Nieratko, Chris 55
Nike skateboards 49, 52
non-traditional skateboarders 34–35,
   37–38
Nordberg, Jenny 8
North American Silly Girl
   Skateboards 29
Nurding, Stefani 63

O'Brien, Jen 29
O'Connor, Paul 81, 83–84
Odanaka, Barbara 19, 35–36
O'Haver, Hanson 36
Oki, Peggy 19, 65
Olive, Rebecca 82, 84
ollie 20, 91–92, *92*
Olympic Games 64, 82–83, 86
O'Neal, Ellen 18, 28
Onto Sneakers 46
Ophelia (character) 6–8
Ortner, Sherry 74
Othman, Mohammed 99

Palestinian House of Friendship 87
Pappalardo, Anthony 28, 104–105
Pappas, Tas 71–72
Parker, Jamie 29
Parviainen, Jaana 72
Pastrana, Lyn-z Adams Hawkins 105
Pavlidis, Adele 1, 71
Pearson, Daniel 76
Penny, Tom 10
Penthouse 25

114   *Index*

Peralta, Stacey 2, 9–10, 22
Percovich, Oliver 99
performances of power 56–57
periphery separatism 46–49
Perry, Bruce 90
Peters, Duane 71, 95
Phelps, Jake 104–105
Philips, Robert 6
physical culture: appearance of falls 69; authentic individualism and 71; bodily-kinaesthetic intelligence and 72–73, 75, 77; distinctive practice and 63; downhill racing 62; gender identity and 63–64, 76; hill bombing 62; influence of surfing on 65–67; injuries and 68–69, 76–77; liquid 65–67; masculinity and 69–70, 73, 76; origin myth of 65–67; plurality in 62; social media visibility and 67–68, 70; struggle and risk-taking in 67–69, 76; symbolism in 106; technique and 70–72, 77; transcending bodily limits and 67–70; transition practice and 62; transport and 62; trick repertoires 62–63; undercutting stoic display in 69–70, 77
Pipher, Mary 7
Pippus, Joel 90
Plan B 27
Please Don't Grab My Boob 45
Plotnick, Danny 34
Pomerantz, Shauna 51–52
Porter, Natalie 2, 22, 28
poser skaters 59n40
post-feminism 58
poststructuralism 38
Powell Peralta 17, 24, 30, 71
Prügl, Elizabeth 57
public space 20, 22, 74–75
punk rock 23–25, 37
Push 52
pushing 91, *92*
Pushing Boarders skateboarding conference 34, 46, 49, 83

queer skateboarding culture 34, 45, 50

Rabelais, François 7
Randy Colvin deck 25

Reagan, Ronald 37
reclaimed separatism 46, 49
Reviving Ophelia (Pipher) 7
Reyes, Jaime 28, 47
Richards, Amy 35
Riot Grrrls 25
Robertson, Edie 18
Rogue Skateboards 29, 32
Romero, Leo 104
Rosa skatepark (Asira Al-Shamalyia) *84, 85, 89, 96*; emotional skills and 90–91; as free open play space 84, 88–89, 93–94, 99; girls-only sessions 98–99; inclusion in 99; participant interviews in 85–86, 90–91, 97; physical/motor skills and 90–91; skateboard philanthropy and 13, 84; social effect of 97
Roy, Georgina 82, 84
Ruiloba, Paola 44

Sablone, Alexis 47
Salinger, J. D. 10
Salmi, Lena 35
Sandoval, Tommy 67
Savage, Emily 24
Sawalha, Mohammed 87
Schechner, Richard 96
Schultz, Christoph Benjamin 6
SDP programmes *see* sport-for-development-and-peace (SDP) programmes
Segovia, Patty 2, 24
Selby, Jenna 29, 32–33
self-expression 96–98
self-knowledge 88–90
separatism 45–49
sexism 48, 104
Shakespeare, William 6
Sherlock, Rachael 44
Sidewalk 31
Sidewalk Surfer 12
Skateboard Annual 18
skateboarder identity: core masculine 9, 11–12, 27, 55, 64, 71; counter-cultural 10; examination of 2; feminal 5–6; femininity and 16; girls and women 2, 5–6, 9; objectification of women and 25; presentation of self and 62

Index 115

Skateboarder Magazine 18, 21
Skateboarder's History of the World (Weyland) 2
skateboard graphics 25–26, 31, *32*
skateboarding: aggressive localism and 36; all-male emphasis in publicity 18; authoritarian relations and 20–22; balance and 93–94; beginnings of 9–10, 36–37; bodily-kinaesthetic intelligence and 72–73, 75; chronology of 16–31; context of sport and 82; dance and 86–87; declines in 22; development of technique 75–76; embodied experience of 88; gender dynamics and 12, 24, 74–75; gender presentations and 1, 3, 62; gestalt therapy and 89; inclusion in 11, 30; influence of surfing on 9, 65–66; mainstreaming of 10, 20; as a nuisance 20–21; physical culture of 2–3; politics and 36–38; poser skaters 59n40; self-expression in 2; self-knowledge in 88–90; smoothness/smoothing of space 93; social-spatial realm 73–76, 106; somatic qualities of 82–83, 86–87, 92–93, 95–96, 106; spatial legitimacy of 22; symbolic movement in 91–93; therapeutic use of 89–91; transition 18, 92; *see also* women skateboarders
Skateboarding (Lombard) 62
skateboarding communities: collective support in 34; communities of practice 49, 74, 76; feminal-oriented 11, 38; gender dynamics and 74–76; genderqueer skateboarders and 38; girl identity in 34–35; girl-made 32–36; non-traditional 34–35; older riders 35–36; skate tours and 34; Southern California 9–10; women and 32–37, 44
skateboarding competitions 29, 33, 46, 62, 64, 103
skateboarding culture: alternative 26, 33–34, 37–38; bodily regulation in 54–56; comedic insults in 56; commercialisation of 103–104; core masculine identity in 9, 11–12,

27, 55, 64, 71; counter-cultural 20–23, 26, 37; critical self-awareness and 27–28, 105; deconstructing 106; feminal 5, 106; gender-blind perspective 48; gender equity and 106; gender politics of 28; heterosexual agency in 27; idealised gender in 50; mainstream culture and 22; male-dominated 18, 23–24; masculinity and 19, 51; movement in 12–13, 91–92; objectification of women in 25–27; outsider positionality in 10–11; peer-to-peer teaching in 75, 83; punk rock and 23–24, 37; queer 34; racial politics and 28; skateboarder ownership of 50; social media visibility and 63, 67–68; Southern California 16–19; symbolic connection to water 65–67; toxic hetero-masculinity and 50; women in 23, 46–47; *see also* physical culture
skateboarding industry: challenges to status quo in 105–106, 108; critical self-awareness and 27–28; female empowerment and 30–31; masculinity and 45–46, 104–105; objectification of women in 50–51; punk rock and 23; separatist approach to 45–46; sexualisation of women in 25–26, 52–53; shared teams and 29–30; skater-owned 50; sponsorship of women 26, 28–29, 32, 46, 56; women and girls in 33; women-owned 29; women skateboarders in advertising 24, 30–31, 52
Skateboarding is Not a Crime (Davis) 2
skateboarding organisations 11, 29, 32
skateboarding publications 23–24, 26–27
skateboarding style: creative self-expression and 94–96; dance and 73; embodied attitude and 95; flatland tricks 19; freestyle tricks in 19–20, 67; individual 95, 106; value and 95; women skateboarders and 28
Skateboard Moms and the Sisters of Shred 35
skateboard philanthropy: critical awareness and 84–85; generosity

116   *Index*

and 98–99; open self-learning in 84, 88–89, 93–94, 99–100; participant response to 82; prefigurative politics and 83; SDP programmes and 81–82, 84; self-expression in 96–98; self-knowledge in 88–89; skateboarding culture and 83; skateboarding for girls and 86–87; skatepark foundations 71; therapeutic use of skateboarding and 89–90
Skate Girls Tribe 34
Skateism 33, 45
Skateistan 71, 89, 99
Skate Kitchen 24
Skate Like a Girl 34
SkatePal 4, 13, 82–84, 86, 88–89, *94*, 98–99
skateparks: adolescent development and 90; closures of 22–23; communities of practice and 74–75, 77; foundations supporting 71; gender dynamics and 74–75; girls-only sessions 98–99; inclusion in 48–49; male-dominated 47; receptiveness to place in 95–96; as sites of social forum 103; skater confidence and 17, 47–48; skill level and 48–49, 74–75; spatial-social power dynamics in 75
SkateQilya 99
Skater Dater 16–17, 20
Skater Girl (Segovia and Heller) 2
skate witches 34
Skate Witches Zine 34
Skinner Releasing Technique 87
SLAP Magazine 95
Smith, Alana 105
Smith, Philip 74
Smith, Stuart 30–31
smoothness/smoothing of space 93
social justice 38, 83
somatic practice: dance and 82–83, 87, 95; listening in 96; self-knowledge in 88; skateboarding as 82–83, 86–87, 92–93, 95–96, 106; unstructured movement and 100
Soto, Jean 70
Southern California 16–19, 24
Spain, Daphne 74

Spice Girls, The 25
sport-for-development-and-peace (SDP) programmes 81–82, 84
sporting activities 73, 81–82, 86–87, 107
Springer, Kimberley 57
Stalefish (Mortimer) 2
Steamer, Elissa 28, 47–49, 55
Strauberry, Cher 34, 63
Street League Skateboarding 11, 29, 45, 52, 64, 83, 103
street skateboarding: authoritarians and 20–22; influence of surfing on 65–66; kerbs (curbs) in 31; learning at 47; risk-taking and 68; spatial legitimacy of 22; transport and 62
Surfer 18
Surf Ghana 34
surfing 9, 36, 65–66, 82
symbolic movement 91–93

Tancowny, Jamie 104
Tash 52
Tessensohn, Anita 24
Thatcher, Margaret 37
Thomas, Jamie 69
Thornhill Caswell, Laura 16–18, 20, *20*, 21, *21*
Thorpe, Holly 46, 81, 84, 99
Thrasher 23, 45, 63, 103–104
Toffoletti, Kim 38
Tony Hawk Foundation 71
Tony Hawk Foundation Podcast 91
Tony Hawk Pro Skater video games 47, 52, 71
Toy Machine 28, 47
transition skateboarding 18, 92
trans skateboarders 37
trans women skateboarders 34, 63
Transworld Skateboarding 24, 53, 65, 71
trick repertoires 62–63, 91
Trienen, Leaf 24
Triple Crown of Skateboarding 47

Unity Skateboards 38

Vagina Monologues, The (Ensler) 9
Vasconcellos, Nora 53–54
Verghese, Atita 34

Very Old Skateboarders and
  Longboarders 35
Video Days 66

Wang, Emily 90
Welcome Skateboards 29
Welcome to Hell 28
Weyland, Jocko 2
Wheaton, Belinda 82, 84
Whitaker, Lisa 29, 32
White, Shari 34
Whitehead, Cindy 29, 44, 53
Whitley, Peter 91
Whittaker, Lisa 49–50
Willing, Indigo 71
Wilson, Charlene 68
women: exclusion from physical
  activity 107; objectification by
  skateboarders 25–27; objectification
  by skateboarding industry 50–51;
  performativity of restriction and
  106–107; self-owned objectification
  and 25; sexualisation of 25–27
women skateboarders: advertising
  support of 24, 30–31, 52; authentic
  individualism and 51–52; brands
  supporting 24, 29–30; challenges to
  bodily restrictions 106–107; counter-
  cultural identification and 10–11, 20;
  demands for equal prize money 29,
  46; documentation of 32–33; double
  standards for 28; empowerment
  and 30; feminism and 44–45, 51;
  freestyle 23; intersectional feminist
  44; as magazine writers 23–24; male

acceptance of 24, 28, 37, 48–49;
  marketing of 50; older riders 35–36;
  participation of 16–21, 23–24, 28;
  performance style of 28; as role
  models 33; sexism and 48, 104;
  solidarity groups and 37; space-
  making by 17, 23–24, 32–33, 49, 57;
  sponsorship of 26, 28–29, 32, 46,
  56; support for 25; *see also* feminal
  skateboarders
Women's Skateboarding Alliance 11, 29
Women's Skateboard Network 24
Woodward, Kath 1
Woozy, Kim 32–33
World Cup of Skateboarding 47
World Industries 25, 27
Wosinska, Magda 63
Wright, E. Missy 10

Xem Skaters 38
X Games 11, 29, 45, 52, 103–104

Yochim, Emily Chivers 19
Young, Iris Marion 106–107

Z-boys *see* Zephyr Team (Z-boys)
Zephyr Team (Z-boys): backyard ramps
  and 18, 22; core practice of 9–10;
  development of skateboarding and
  18–20, 24, 36; physical styles of
  19–20, 66–67; pool-riding and
  19–20, 65; as surfer-skateboarders 9,
  65; transition skateboarding and 18
Zero Skateboard 67, 69
Zimmerschneider, Rachel 56

Taylor & Francis eBooks

www.taylorfrancis.com

A single destination for eBooks from Taylor & Francis with increased functionality and an improved user experience to meet the needs of our customers.

90,000+ eBooks of award-winning academic content in Humanities, Social Science, Science, Technology, Engineering, and Medical written by a global network of editors and authors.

TAYLOR & FRANCIS EBOOKS OFFERS:

- A streamlined experience for our library customers
- A single point of discovery for all of our eBook content
- Improved search and discovery of content at both book and chapter level

REQUEST A FREE TRIAL
support@taylorfrancis.com

Milton Keynes UK
Ingram Content Group UK Ltd.
UKHW030712231124
451456UK00027B/371